Margo Murray

Beyond the Myths and Magic of Mentoring

How to Facilitate an Effective Mentoring Process

New and Revised Edition

JOSSEY-BASS
A Wiley Company
www.josseybass.com

Published by

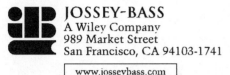

JOSSEY-BASS
A Wiley Company
989 Market Street
San Francisco, CA 94103-1741

www.josseybass.com

Jossey-Bass books and products are available through most bookstores. To contact Jossey-Bass directly, call (888) 378-2537, fax to (800) 605-2665, or visit our website at www.josseybass.com.

Substantial discounts on bulk quantities of Jossey-Bass books are available to corporations, professional associations, and other organizations. For details and discount information, contact the special sales department at Jossey-Bass.

We at Jossey-Bass strive to use the most environmentally sensitive paper stocks available to us. Our publications are printed on acid-free recycled stock whenever possible, and our paper always meets or exceeds minimum GPO and EPA requirements.

Library of Congress Cataloging-in-Publication Data

Murray, Margo, 1935-
    Beyond the myths and magic of mentoring : how to facilitate an effective mentoring process / Margo Murray.—New and rev. ed.
        p. cm.—(The Jossey-Bass business & management series)
    Includes bibliographical references and index.
    ISBN 0-7879-5675-9
    1. Mentoring in business. I. Title. II. Series.
    HF5385 .M8575 2001
    658.3'124—dc21   00-012933

SECOND EDITION
HB Printing   10 9 8 7 6 5 4

The Jossey-Bass

Business & Management Series

To my first mentor, Marcus Hanna Murray,
and to Charles Bell and Albert Ellison,
who modeled the role in facilitated processes

In this second edition I must add
Howard H. McFann, Ph.D., mentor,
who helped me learn more
than I really ever wanted to know
about learning and evaluation

Contents

Preface

Every week I get calls from people who say, "I'm reading your book *Beyond the Myths and Magic of Mentoring*, and it is *so* helpful." My usual response is, "Well, I'm a lot smarter today than when I wrote that book!"

It is a different world in so many ways. Organizations are leaner, flatter, and sometimes described as meaner. The surplus labor pool has dried up, and in many countries there is a critical shortage of skilled workers. The dot com businesses and stock market gains have made instant millionaires of many people. The thirty-something employees want more than a job—and certainly are not seeking long-term careers. They will change jobs seven or more times during their career life, sometimes just to be where they feel appreciated.

Many people in the United States complain that they are working more hours, feeling more stress, and lacking work and life balance. In fact, workers in this country have the shortest vacations and the least number of holidays of any country I know of. When I ask people why they are working so hard, it becomes evident that most really like what they are doing. It is a matter of choice among priorities for many. Others are caught in the economics of the spiraling costs of housing, transportation, and child care, which necessitate at least two jobs per household. With the stress of pressure to become productive more quickly, people want help in moving up the learning curve more efficiently.

The hierarchical organization is disappearing as more people work in communities, or on project or engagement teams. Rather than looking to a mentoring process to groom people for upward movement or greater responsibility, many organizations today want to have a mentoring process as visible evidence of concern and caring for their employees. Lacking the blind loyalty of their predecessors, these workers want to be recognized as people, and for their contributions.

Recruitment, retention, and creating a more diverse workforce are the primary drivers for mentoring processes now. In a recent survey, I learned that career development was the focus for 42 percent of 636 pairs of mentors and protégés. Other organizations are looking to mentoring as a strategy to improve competitiveness with increased productivity. Another 30 percent of the pairs I surveyed had been matched for technical skills transfer. The focus was to pass on state-of-the-art knowledge and skills from expert hires, or to create a multiskilled and flexible workforce. My vision is that every organization will have mentoring as a part of the culture. New employees, whether hired as entry-level craft or clerical, or at the executive or professional level, will have a choice of mentors to help them readily enter the work environment and learn the values, the communication channels, and how things work. The mentoring process will be an intervention of choice. Decision makers will be pleased with the increased cost-effectiveness of enabling people to produce results and will support the process in good times and leaner ones.

I want to share with you in this edition what I have learned in the last ten years about how to make mentoring work effectively. I also want to assure you that I have kept the user-friendly format and timeless guidelines that made the first edition so helpful. The clients with whom we have worked certainly helped to hone those guidelines, and the improvements are included in this edition— and appreciated. I am pleased to be able to draw on our work with implementing mentoring processes to give you examples of best practices with particular guidelines. In recent publications, I found many examples of how people are using the guidelines and strategies described in the earlier edition of this book. Those examples prove it is beyond magic!

Now for some lessons learned. Here is what I have learned about what *not* to do in implementing a mentoring process:

- Do not start a process unless you intend to seriously work it for two or three years to make it part of the culture.
- Do not skip the readiness assessment step; the process will not survive without the ongoing support of at least one top manager or administrator.
- Do not introduce it as a training event.
- Do not make it exclusive to one group of people.
- Do not expect it to administer itself.
- Do not permit divisions or functions to set up individual programs and fragment scarce resources.
- Do not let the mentors convince you that they don't need "training" for their role.
- Do not expect all coaching and feedback to be effective when done by electronic communication; a nonverbal message is essential for some interaction.
- Do not promise people they will have time to work with their mentors, and then switch priorities at the last minute; they will cease to trust you.

Don't panic with this list of the pitfalls. Just a little further on in this section, I give you a list of what I have found to be the critical success factors of an implementation. More good news is that in this book you find excellent examples of how people have hurdled these obstacles and made the process pay off. The examples come from all kinds of industry in the public sector, from nonprofit groups, and from education at all levels. People are making mentoring work. Some of the most exciting work we have done is with youths in both high-potential and at-risk groups. As I was completing this manuscript, I had an exciting conversation with Don Gray (e-mail to author, Sept. 7, 2000), with whom we worked on the pilot of the mentoring component of the AYES School-to-Career initiative (described in Chapter One). His enthusiastic acknowledgement of the value of the mentoring process for these students and their mentors was music to my ears. I hope that enthusiasm, and the AYES-model initiative, continues to spread around the globe to young people in many career pursuits.

I continue to recognize my own experience with accelerated promotion processes in two large organizations as the genesis for my design of facilitated mentoring. Those early experiences gave me a glimpse of what mentoring could be. Inspired by my own good and bad mentoring experiences, and stimulated by the assessed needs of the organizations with which I worked, I developed the Facilitated Mentoring Model and tested it in several of the line and operational functions that I managed. By early 1971, I had enough of the framework in place to use it to share the concept with people who were interested in exploring a mentoring process. As the work progressed, longitudinal studies with client groups and research of others' experiences produced criteria, guidelines, and formats for each component of the model. For almost thirty years, I have systematically analyzed and used feedback from all participants in mentoring processes—coordinators, mentors, protégés, and bosses—to refine the model and processes. I believe we have now proven the value of mentoring as a performance improvement intervention.

What Is Mentoring?

What is this phenomenon called *mentoring?* In Gary B. Trudeau's popular comic strip *Doonesbury*, Cassie says to Mike, "I didn't even know it was a verb" (1984). Well, it isn't a verb, although many people still use both *mentor* and *mentoring* in this way. Scott Adams has a Dilbert character saying of a bungee boss, "He was like a mentor to me" (Adams, 1994). Misconceptions still abound about who a mentor is and what a mentor does. Are all the writers of articles on mentoring describing the same type of relationship and activity? I think not. Here is the definition of *mentoring* used in this book:

Mentoring is a deliberate pairing of a more skilled or more experienced person with a less skilled or less experienced one, with the mutually agreed goal of having the less skilled person grow and develop specific competencies

Most recent articles on mentoring describe situations in which a person has been positively influenced by another; I would call the latter a *role model* rather than a mentor. The influencer may not even have known that he or she was viewed as someone to emulate. The distant star who attracts a number of imitators is not a mentor, by my definition, because only the imitators know of the influence. An influential person may also affect the growth or career of another by acting as a *sponsor*. For example, when an opportunity for promotion or a plum assignment opens up, the sponsor mentions the name of a favored person. In these cases, the sponsors know what they are doing; however, the beneficiaries may be totally unaware of the support or favors given. In contrast, a mentor and protégé enter into an overt agreement to interact in certain ways to facilitate the learning, growth, and skill development of either or both of them.

Now for the list of the critical success factors that I promised. First, I continue to make a clear distinction between facilitated mentoring and other forms of structured or formal mentoring. *Facilitated mentoring* is an elegantly simple and flexible structure and series of processes designed to create effective mentoring relationships; guide the desired behavior change of those involved; and evaluate the results for the protégés, the mentors, and the organization. A facilitated mentoring process typically includes these components:

- A design that supports the assessed goals and perceived needs of the organization
- Criteria and a process for selecting priority groups of protégés
- Strategies and tools for diagnosing the developmental needs of protégés

- Criteria and a process for qualifying mentors
- Strategies for matching mentors and protégés on the basis of skills to be developed and compatibility
- Orientation on the responsibilities of the role for both mentors and protégés
- Preparation of the participants for a healthy, productive relationship
- A negotiated agreement among mentor, protégé, and (if appropriate) the boss
- A coordination team responsible for maintaining the process and supporting the relationships
- Formative evaluation to continuously improve the process
- Summative evaluation to determine outcomes for the organization, the mentors, and the protégés

Many kinds of mentoring processes exist in a variety of organizations and appear to meet particular needs. A pairing of peers for mutual support may in effect be mentoring, but I would not call this a facilitated mentoring process. It is more of a "buddy" arrangement, which serves a useful enough purpose to many people, especially new hires to a company.

As is implied in our definition of *mentoring,* the primary purpose of facilitated mentoring is to systematically develop the skills and leadership abilities of the less experienced members of an organization. Facilitated mentoring is appropriate when an organization wants to cause this growth and development to happen and wants to know that it has. A true learning organization uses mentoring as a strategy for continuously upgrading the knowledge and skills of all employees. Whether the organization is for-profit or nonprofit, the bottom line is improved results, such as increased productivity, increased quality of service, reduced costs, stakeholder value, or fidelity to donors' purposes. (The benefits to the organization and how to realize them are described in Chapter Three.)

Purpose of the Book

People often ask me, "How did you get interested in facilitated mentoring anyway? What makes you believe in it so strongly? How can I structure a mentoring process and make it work?" This book is my answer to these questions.

When we look at the plethora of publications on mentoring, it becomes obvious that journalists and not practitioners write most of them. As I scanned two file boxes of such articles to find evidence of results to include here, the number of articles that merely repeated data from other articles was striking. We at MMHA The Managers' Mentors, Inc., repeatedly encourage our clients to write about their lessons learned and best practices, and we invite them to conferences to present their experiences. This book includes many examples of real experiences, both good and bad, with mentoring processes and relationships. I have also gathered current research and information on others' experiences with mentoring. The primary purpose remains to illustrate various models of facilitated mentoring and to offer specific guidelines for assessing the need for such a process in an organization and for designing and implementing it. The models described in Part Two include the best designs of a viable facilitated mentoring process.

Audience

The intended audiences for this book are planners, operating managers, learning administrators, and human resource professionals in any type of industrial, government, health care, nonprofit, or educational organization (small or large). If you have the first edition and are scanning this in a book store (or have lifted it from a colleague's desk!), go ahead and buy your own copy. I promise you there is enough new material here to save you a lot of time. Your time is valuable, and this might just get you an extra day off.

For those people who want to be a mentor or find a mentor, this book has helpful information on mentoring relationships and how to make them work. If you are or want to be a mentor, I suggest you look particularly at these chapters:

Chapter One ("What Mentoring Is—and What It Is Not")

Chapter Two ("Mentoring at Work in Organizations")

Chapter Three ("The Upside and the Downside for the Organization")

Chapter Five ("The Mentor's Motivation and Concerns")

Chapter Eight ("Structuring the Mentor Role: Qualifications, Recruitment, Selection, and Rewards")

Chapter Ten ("Involving the Boss Who Is Not the Mentor")

Chapter Twelve ("Negotiating Sound Mentoring Agreements")

Chapter Fourteen ("Gender, Culture, and Relationship Concerns")

Chapter Fifteen ("Making Facilitated Mentoring Work")

The most relevant reading for protégés is in these chapters:

Chapter One ("What Mentoring Is—and What It Is Not")

Chapter Four ("Payoffs and Penalties for the Protégé")

Chapter Nine ("Selecting Protégés and Diagnosing Their Development Needs")

Chapter Ten ("Involving the Boss Who Is Not the Mentor")

Chapter Twelve ("Negotiating Sound Mentoring Agreements")

Chapter Fourteen ("Gender, Culture, and Relationship Concerns")

Chapter Fifteen ("Making Facilitated Mentoring Work")

If you are considering mentoring as a strategy for improving the results of your organization, the guidelines in this book help you determine whether your organization is ready for a facilitated mentoring process. You will find meaningful answers to these questions:

- What is the gap that facilitated mentoring fills?
- What outcomes and benefits can be derived from facilitating the relationships?

- Can mentoring be structured and still be flexible?
- Is our organization ready for such a process?
- How big must the organization be to gain cost benefit?
- Can the results be measured?
- How does mentoring fit with other interventions?
- Where do you place the mentoring function in the organization?
- Who administers the process?
- What skills are required on the coordination team?
- How do you budget for it?
- How are mentors prepared?
- How are protégés selected?

The guidelines, examples, and checklists show you how to tailor a mentoring process for your own organization. If you have a process in place, those guidelines and checklists enable you to audit and improve it.

How This Book Is Designed and Organized

The second edition of *Beyond the Myths and Magic of Mentoring* is designed to give you quick access to the information you need most. You do not have to read it from front to back. For example, if you are ready to implement a facilitated mentoring process, you can get on with it by skipping to Chapter Six. There you will find detailed descriptions of each component of a facilitated mentoring model. Then proceed to Chapters Seven through Thirteen, where the specifics of mentor and protégé selection, coordinator responsibilities, negotiated agreements, and evaluation are illustrated. Because of this design, readers who do choose to read from cover to cover will find some key information repeated. Scan through the chapter descriptions here and find those that best suit your needs.

- The first two chapters trace the evolution of mentoring, from early Greek mythology to the present. I have included a brief reference from an article that Fred Nickols suggested I read (Roberts, 1999), which suggested that the original Mentor was not very good at his job. I also give reasons an increasing number of organizations are implementing mentoring processes.

- Chapter One gives a brief history of the term *mentor*, discusses terminology used in mentoring processes, and defines what I mean by mentoring in this book. Chapter Two relates the experiences of some people who have benefited from a mentoring relationship to illustrate the broad spectrum of mentor-protégé interaction, describes trends in how mentoring is being used in organizations, and cites some of the motives for the increasing interest in facilitated mentoring processes.

- The next three chapters look at what's in it for everybody— and what might go wrong. If you have your own list of pros and cons, this section is an opportunity to compare your issues and others' experiences. Chapter Three looks at the benefits the organization can gain and the potential problems it faces when implementing a mentoring process. Chapter Four discusses the positive and negative aspects of the mentoring relationship for the protégé. Chapter Five explains why a person would willingly take on the role of mentor; it also lists stumbling blocks that mentors and the organization must guard against.

- In Chapter Six, models and descriptions of processes structured for the public sector, private industry, health care, and educational institutions are presented along with a generic implementation flow of a facilitated mentoring process. You may find it helpful to scan these illustrations before reading further in the book to become familiar with the components included in a typical facilitated mentoring process. Chapter Six illustrates the key elements recommended for a facilitated mentoring process, examines the operating concept of a facilitated mentoring process and its role relationships, and presents

PREFACE xix

six applications of other facilitated mentoring processes used in the public and private sectors, with brief annotation of the activity in each component of that mentoring process.

- Chapters Seven through Twelve feature detailed guidelines for designing, implementing, and coordinating a facilitated mentoring process. The material here can be a primary resource for anyone who may be involved as a process designer, evaluator, coordinator, mentor, or protégé. You can use the checklist at the end of each of these chapters to gather the data needed to make important decisions about implementing facilitated mentoring in your organization.

- Chapter Seven discusses how to decide whether a mentoring process fills an identified gap, and whether the culture of the organization supports such a process. Chapter Eight gives tips on mentor qualifications and recruitment and on making the mentoring role work. Chapter Nine outlines strategies for identifying protégé candidates and suggests criteria for selecting protégés; it then explains the importance of individual development planning and how to do it. Chapter Ten lists problems likely to be encountered in the mentor-protégé-boss triangle and outlines how to make the relationship work comfortably. Chapter Eleven describes the coordination team's responsibilities and discusses the skills that coordination team members need. Chapter Twelve suggests areas in which parameters must be set in the mentor-protégé agreement and explains what do when the agreement doesn't work.

- Chapter Thirteen describes issues in evaluation, gives how-tos for designing evaluations, and discusses which outcomes might be tracked and how to track them. Chapter Fourteen discusses how differences in sex, race, and age can be beneficial to the mentor-protégé relationship, suggests realistic approaches for dealing with relationship problems when they come up, and discusses several objections that may be expressed by others in the organization (mentoring is too costly; it causes jealousy; it produces clones). Chapter Fifteen shares some current experiences and best practices, and it summarizes my recommendations for using facilitated mentoring in organizations.

Acknowledgments

How can I give credit to so many people who have shared parts of my vision and enriched my life? There are many whose special support must be acknowledged. I continue to be grateful to all those who contributed to the first edition: Marna, Kathe, Karen, Roger, Marcy, Russell, Mike, and Walt. One of my special mentors has since crossed over, and I know he continues to guide some of my better thinking.

I often tell mentors who are new to the role that they are about to have the richest and most rewarding experience of their lives. Every day, I experience that richness with the MMHA associates around the world who have contributed greatly to upgrading the concept and practice of facilitated mentoring.

All the clients in the more than one hundred organizations with whom I have collaborated and learned about the art and craft of improving work performance deserve special gratitude for making the mentoring process contribute to their improved results.

This edition has been considerably improved by the discerning eyes and helpful input of Launa Craig, Kathe Rickel, and Wendy Lindstrom. Only they know of the pressure placed on us when I agreed to an aggressive deadline. Perhaps the greatest gift of all is that of friendship; I am blessed to have in my life longtime friends Jethna, Elsie and Roland, Scott, Susan, Mary and Dick, and others who will not be named but know who they are.

I would also like to thank the Jossey-Bass editors and staff for their support and encouragement—especially Susan Williams, who finally managed to convince me this update was necessary.

Oakland, California   Margo Murray
December 2000

The Author

Margo Murray is president and chief operating officer of MMHA The Managers' Mentors, Inc., an international consulting firm established in 1974. She received a B.S. degree (1963) from California State University, Sacramento, in business administration; and her M.B.A. (1977) from John F. Kennedy University in advanced management theory.

Murray's main research and professional contributions have been in organizational needs assessment and in analyzing, designing, developing, implementing, and evaluating performance systems. Her innovations include originating the facilitated mentoring process and applying a criterion-referenced approach to management skill development. Models and resources she created are used in public and private organizations worldwide. She has authored dozens of published programs and articles that have won professional awards (as well as White House recognition for excellence) and been translated into several languages.

Murray was elected in 1965 to Beta Gamma Sigma, the national honor society in business, for her graduate research. In 1979 she was honored as an Outstanding Member of the National Society for Performance and Instruction; in 1984 was awarded its highest honor, Member for Life; and she served as president in 1986–1987. In 1988 the alumni association of California State University, Sacramento, recognized her "innovative contributions to her profession both nationally and internationally and her creative leadership and dedication to promoting strong mentoring programs" with the Distinguished Service Award; in 1998 the school recognized her as Alum of the Year. In 1998 the International Federation of Training and Development Organisations awarded her an honorary membership, only the third ever granted by the IFTDO.

Murray's management and consulting skills were honed in line and staff positions with Pacific Telephone and in management information systems and as a budget officer with the U.S. Air Force. She serves on the board of the International Mentoring Association, and formerly on the boards of the University of San Francisco McLaren School of Business, the IFTDO, and the board of regents of John F. Kennedy University.

Part One

The Mentoring Concept, Benefits, and Pitfalls

Part One begins by tracing the evolution of the mentoring concept as it is described in mythological, religious, popular, and research literature. You may wish to skip the first two chapters if you have already decided to implement a mentoring process and are less interested in the history than in the how-tos.

Chapter One describes the evolution and language of mentoring. It discusses what mentoring is and what it isn't at this stage of the evolutionary process. Keep in mind, the strategies used in mentoring processes are changing every day as we examine lessons learned and best practices. The roles of those involved in various mentoring processes are described as a framework for understanding the components of a facilitated mentoring process.

To illustrate the many ways in which a mentor and protégé interact, Chapter Two describes the experiences of and quotes from a few notable people who have commented on the benefits they received from a mentoring relationship. The examples were selected to dispel the myth that mentoring is a rare, magical happening.

Those quoted are or were engaged in the arts, sciences, and industry; yet they all credit a mentoring experience for preparing them for their life's work.

It is probably safe to say that every organization has benefited from the contribution of a person who was stimulated by a mentoring relationship. The question "How many of you have had a helpful mentor?" when posed to thousands of people in our presentations and workshops on mentoring has always elicited a positive response from a high percentage of participants. A sparkle comes to the eye at recollection of the magic of these exceptional relationships. Admittedly the sample is biased; however, our literature searches and individual interview data support this conclusion. In the past ten years, popular journals and magazines have reported many examples of informal mentoring that have met with varying degrees of success. More of them now support the strategy of facilitating the process rather than leaving it to chance. Chapter Two relates some noteworthy experiences from my own work and current publications.

Chapter Two describes a number of motives for the increasing interest in facilitating mentoring processes. Some managers and administrators still believe it is impossible to structure this process, accepting the theory that the relationship is more likely to jell if it happens spontaneously. Nevertheless, we have now consulted with more than one hundred organizations that are proving the feasibility of facilitating the mentoring process in systematic ways with good results. (Several of those organizations have generously contributed examples from their own programs for Chapter Six, and relevant comments from clients are cited in other chapters.) The structure of a mentoring process and the extent to which the strategies of mentoring processes are formalized depend on

- The needs of the organization
- The philosophy of human resource development within it
- The availability of other developmental resources

The viewpoints of the organization, the protégé, and the mentor toward the mentoring relationship are described in Chapters Three, Four, and Five. These chapters are filled with examples of issues and benefits for each of these participants. As you consider using mentors to facilitate continuous learning in your organization, you will no doubt think of many obstacles you may face in implementation. As one of these "yes, but . . ." thoughts pops into your mind, jot it down in the margin of the book. Chapters Seven through Twelve give you many preventive strategies for overcoming these obstacles.

Part One of this book serves two purposes: to review the value of healthy mentoring relationships and to give you some language to use and examples to cite in explaining mentoring to others. If you are already sold on the concept of mentoring and confident of your ability to describe it to others, you may wish to skip to Part Two and get on with preparing to design or audit your own process.

Chapter One

What Mentoring Is—and What It Is Not

If we are to believe the media and literature, literally hundreds of organizations have implemented some type of mentoring program in the past ten years. Millions of people from primary school to almost retirement age are in mentoring relationships. What is fascinating is that there are still two basic schools of thought about mentoring. One is the belief that mentoring can be structured or facilitated; the other is the belief that it can only "happen," to a lucky or aggressive few people.

In an attempt to bring some understanding of various processes called mentoring, and to allow comparison of features of informal and facilitated, I coined this definition:

> *Facilitated mentoring* is a structure and series of processes designed to create effective mentoring relationships; guide the desired behavior change of those involved; and evaluate the results for the protégés, the mentors, and the organization.

The primary purpose of a facilitated mentoring process is to systematically develop the skills and competencies of the less experienced people. To clarify the relationship of mentoring to other modes of training and development, it may be helpful to define some other terms. I define *learning* as an observable change in behavior, and I define *training* as the process of helping someone learn. Training can occur through using self-study texts, interactive videodisc modules, and so on; prepared instruction is delivered online through a computer or through modeling, tutoring, and coaching by a mentor or trainer.

Our experience suggests that a process, such as a mentoring process, for helping someone learn cannot be mandated or made to work solely by structural change. It is essential to have behavior change in the decision makers and participants in order to realize the potential benefits. A facilitated mentoring process in the organization (public, private, or nonprofit) can create conditions for motivating such changes in behavior. In addition, a planned mentoring process has a great advantage over happenstance matches: by structuring and facilitating the pairings, we can prevent the problems that are likely to occur with mismatches. Problems occur in the best of relationships, and a facilitator can assist with solving the problems while protecting the beneficial relationship. Finally, organizations can gather data to track results, measure outcomes, and assess the cost effectiveness of a facilitated mentoring process.

Today there are fewer representatives of the second school of thought, who suggest that true mentoring is spontaneous or informal, and who caution that it cannot be structured or formalized. Some still hold the opinion that a structured mentoring relationship lacks a critical, magical ingredient. They see it as an arranged marriage—utilitarian but often lacking passion. Fury (1980) wrote that the mentor-protégé relationship is a "mysterious, chemical attraction of two people . . . prompt[ing] them to take the risks inherent in any intensely close relationship" (p. 47). Early researchers who attempted objective studies of mentoring relationships tended to paint a dismal picture of the prospects of guiding the process. In a report of a two-year study, Premac Associates (1984, p. 55) concluded, "Mentoring . . . seems to work best when it is simply 'allowed to happen.' "

The increasing number of participants in what others call formal programs presents strong evidence against that opinion. I cite the results of organizations' facilitated mentoring processes in relevant places in this second edition. David Clutterbuck (1995) concludes that formality is a necessity within mentoring programs, but that the amount of formality needs to be flexible and determined by the company to fit its own needs. To emphasize the importance of maintaining the magic of the pairing while avoiding the stifling effect of excessive structure, I have chosen to use the term *facilitated:* the organization facilitates the beneficial results for the mentor, the protégé, and the organization itself. When describing my research and experience, I use the term *facilitated.* When relating the experience of others, I use their terms—*formal, structured,* or *informal*—with clarifying notations where necessary.

More on the language of mentoring and the terms used in this book later in this chapter; for now let's go back to the genesis of the concept.

Evolution of Mentoring

History gives many examples of the value of mentoring. Perhaps the most famous instance was chronicled by Homer in *The Odyssey.* Homer tells us that around 1200 B.C., the adventurer Odysseus made ready to leave for the siege of Troy. Before sailing, he appointed a guardian to his household. For the next ten years, this guardian acted faithfully as teacher, adviser, friend, and surrogate father to Telemachus, son of Odysseus. The mythical guardian's name was Mentor.

Homer's story reflects one of the oldest attempts by a society to facilitate mentoring. It was customary in ancient Greece for young male citizens to be paired with older males in the hope that each boy would learn and emulate the values of his mentor, usually a friend of the boy's father or a relative. The Greeks premised these relationships on a basic principle of human survival: Humans learn skills, culture, and values directly from other humans whom they look up to or admire.

From a fresh return to Homer's *Odyssey,* Andy Roberts suggests that "Mentor . . . was simply an old friend of King Ulysses who largely failed in his duties of keeping the King's household intact." Roberts goes on to say it was "the goddess Pallas Athene . . . who took Mentor's form so as to guide, counsel, and enable both Odysseus and his son Telemachus through their journey" (1999, pp. 81, 90). Roberts describes Homer's Mentor as far removed from the caring, nurturing Mentor of myth and argues that the commonplace view of the Mentor who counsels, guides, nurtures, advises, and enables is owed not to Homer but to Fénelon, a fifteenth-century French cleric and author of *Les Aventures de Télémaque*, an imitation or continuation of the epic *Odyssey*. Fénelon's rich descriptions of Mentor may well account for the word *mentor* appearing in the *Oxford English Dictionary* as a common noun, cited as first used in 1750.

How much of your current behavior stems from interactions with your parents or parental figures? Have you ever stopped in midsentence and thought with mock horror, "I sound just like my parents!"? This is evidence of how powerful modeling is and can be. Children learn to avoid physical harm through parental warnings and example. They learn to communicate and interact primarily in the family unit. If the interactions are healthy, then successful and valuable behavior is copied and repeated. Unfortunately, unpleasant or destructive behavior is just as likely to be repeated. Humans tend to emulate the behavior they see in others, especially when that behavior is rewarded (Bandura, 1986). Successive generations of family members carry on many of the behaviors and rituals modeled by parents and parental figures.

These same principles of modeling and mentoring have been key elements in the continuity of art, craft, and commerce from ancient times. A good example can be found in the craft guilds that began in the Middle Ages. These societies helped structure the professions of merchant, lawyer, goldsmith, and others. Young boys were traditionally apprenticed to a master, a person who was considered excellent in his trade and who owned a shop or business. The boy lived with the master, worked his way up to journeyman, and finally became a master himself by taking an examination or producing an exemplary work in his profession (hence the word *masterpiece*). Often the new master would take over the business at the old master's retirement or death. It was also traditional for him to marry the master's widow and take over the family responsibilities. Through this form of structured mentoring, the craft guilds controlled the quality of work and the wages of their professions and passed on valuable social and political considerations.

The master-apprentice relationship was eventually transformed into the employer-employee relationship by industrial society. Employers' focus shifted away from maintaining quality and tradition toward increasing their profits. What benefited the master no longer benefited the apprentice. Lower wages and longer work hours eventually gave birth to the unions. The turbulent era of worker against management was born.

Informal mentoring has its place in history as well. Academic research, popular literature, and personal accounts tout the value of informal mentoring in every conceivable vocation and avocation. Protégés describe the magical richness of these developmental exchanges in glowing generalities. Mary Cassatt reported (McMullen, 1984, p. 293) what it meant to her when the Impressionist artist Edgar Degas took a personal interest in her professional career and became her mentor: "I accepted with joy. Now I could work with absolute independence without considering the opinion of a jury. I had already recognized who were my true masters. I admired Manet, Courbet, and Degas. I took leave of conventional art. I began to live."

In such historical informal relationships, the mentor may have assisted in career advancement or guided the protégé through the political pathways of a profession or an organization. Less frequently, the contact may have included coaching the protégé in developing specific skills. No matter how minimal or extensive, this individual attention almost always had positive results for the protégé, such as increased professional recognition or job effectiveness. For the mentor, a sense of accomplishment came from having made a contribution to the growth of another person.

Since the mid-1970s great attention has been paid to both informal and facilitated mentoring relationships and their impact in the business world. As companies grow leaner, flatter, and more impersonal, their need for person-to-person mentoring grows. In fact, mentoring has been described as "an American management innovation" (Odiorne, 1985, p. 63). For a company to survive and thrive, it must have a mechanism for regenerating itself from within. At Hewlett-Packard's Roseville Division, employees who request a mentor are being matched with high-level managers who assist in coaching in subjects ranging anywhere from public speaking to negotiation techniques. Employees specify what skills they want to learn and are then paired with a mentor (Ferraro, 1995).

The structured program at SC Johnson Wax pairs new employees with those already established within the company. One participant in the program, Darian Griffin, says, "Mentoring programs can help you understand the inner workings of the company and draw on the experiences of someone who's already gone through what you're going through. It gave me a chance to get my career goals buttoned down and determine what things I can work on to achieve those goals" ("Formal Mentoring Program," 1996). Many companies have developed similar programs focused on other corporate initiatives such as succession planning and technical skills transfer.

Mentoring is no longer associated only with women and other underrepresented groups. The competitiveness of the global economy is reuniting the values of worker and manager; both are beginning to recognize the need for leadership and quality. A program at DuPont is determined to work effectively to "preserve institutional memory and intellectual capital" and allows the staff members to personally choose their mentors from a list that details each manager's skills and experience (Jossi, 1997). Many organizations support the mentoring process and put in place structures and procedures for carrying out facilitated mentoring for all employees who seek new skills and knowledge. At Sony (Akio Morita, interview with author, 1988), for example, all new employees wear a small green circle on their identification badges. The green circle tells experienced employees to stop and give their full attention to the new employee, to share know-how and the ways of the corporate culture. Akio Morita, the now-deceased chairman of the board of Sony, had a clear vision of the role this philosophy played in Sony's success (Morita, 1988): "We are making ourselves responsible for their education and well-being. I consider it my job as a manager to do everything I can to nurture the curiosity of people I work with" (p. 2).

Another exciting example is the Automotive Youth Education System (AYES) school-to-career initiative, which pairs secondary school students with master service technicians in automotive dealerships. Donald I. Gray calls the mentoring component "the linchpin of our AYES model. Our mentoring process has set the AYES initiative apart from all other automotive training programs" (e-mail to author, Sept. 7, 2000).

Does the ancient concept of mentoring have its place in today's modern business world? In the technology driven twenty-first century, the need for facilitated mentoring is greater than ever. Organizations are still made up of people—people who require ever greater skills for mastering the increasingly complex issues and tasks in every working environment. The complexity of today's organizations, coupled with increasing emphasis on cost containment, makes facilitated mentoring an attractive, low-cost strategy for developing and keeping a skilled workforce.

It is true that the chemistry of many informal mentoring experiences cannot be automatically created through structure. Best practices now prove that facilitated mentoring can give a protégé the same opportunity offered the apprentice of medieval times: a chance to learn from a master. Caring managers can readily design strategies for encouraging the richness and magic in a relationship. Magic and chemistry? Well, most magicians have a skillful assistant, and the most productive chemical research has always been carried on in carefully controlled environments. Assisting, guiding, and controlling the mentoring process have proven to be feasible in historical and modern times. Is it worth the effort? Using the data and guidelines in this book, you will be able to answer that question for your organization and for yourself.

Language of Mentoring

Hennig and Jardim advised ambitious (contemporary) women to "look for a coach, a godfather or godmother, a mentor, and advocate" (1977, p. 162), and Levinson (1986) suggested the terms *coach, adviser, senior adviser, counselor,* and *experience leader.* The mentor has also at times been designated as the *master, guide, exemplar, luminary, trainer, instructor, leader,* and *boss.*

Mentor seems to be an acceptable term today; we see it used in business, education, government, and nonprofit organizations all over the world. Even so, when translating from English to other languages we are sometimes offered words that have undesirable connotations, requiring a search for an acceptable synonym. What's in a name? The titles given to the various roles in a mentoring process can reflect the organization's philosophy, style, and culture. The culture of an organization determines the titles that are most acceptable for each of the roles, particularly that of mentor. (*Culture* is defined here as the shared beliefs and biases that shape the way people are treated in an organization.)

We can use the word *coach* to demonstrate the link between company culture and mentoring terminology. *Coach* has become a popular term for the mentor role in companies concerned with productivity and competition. *Partner* is a term used in companies that focus on collaboration. With the rapid growth of the coaching profession, we are often asked how mentoring and coaching differ. The key point is that mentor is not something a person does; rather, it describes the *role* assumed by one willing to help another to learn and grow. Coaching is one of the many activities carried out by the mentor, as are guiding, guarding, and giving feedback. The role, tasks, and skills of mentors are further described in Chapter Eight.

Because a facilitated mentoring process can be a major investment for an organization of any size, it is unwise to jeopardize the full realization of benefits by choosing an objectionable title for the key players in the process. The discussion here clarifies various titles and describes how they are used in this book. The terms used for the roles performed by those involved in mentoring processes are many and varied. The terms in this book are those used by the organizations providing examples; where appropriate, they are differentiated from the terms used to describe facilitated mentoring in the how-to parts of this book.

Definitions: Who Is and Isn't a Mentor?

Role model, sponsor, and mentor—how are they alike and how do they differ? A careful look at each of these roles gives the answer.

Sponsor

A *sponsor* can be an active booster or advocate for any number of people, all at the same time. For example, a sponsor can finance the company baseball team, recommend several candidates for promotional opportunities, or establish scholarship funds at the local university. A sponsor is constrained only by time and generosity. On the receiving end, a fortunate individual may have several sponsors. The sponsoring relationship is informal, with neither person making any commitments of responsibility or interaction. The sponsor most certainly knows who is being sponsored; however, the sponsored person may or may not know who the sponsor is. The sponsor role can continue indefinitely, as long as the sponsor sees a need and is willing and able to continue in the role. Activities of the sponsor of another individual in the business world include

- Making introductions to top people in the organization
- Making introductions to others with influence in the industry or profession
- Making recommendations for advancement
- Reflecting power on the sponsored person by publicly praising accomplishments and abilities
- Facilitating entry into meetings and activities usually attended by high-level people

- Serving as a confidant
- Offering guidance in the customs of the organization

Role Models

Role models can perform the same activities as a sponsor or can simply be held in high regard by any number of people without even knowing that they are viewed in this favorable light. Undoubtedly, Malcolm Forbes was a role model to hundreds of aspiring business students, whether they'd met him or not. Similarly, an individual may have several role models at one time. There is no particular structure to the role-modeling relationship. It can continue as long as the observer sees positive behaviors to emulate. Role models often exhibit

- Success
- Exemplary behavior in achievement and style
- Ability to get things done
- Knowledge of organization policy and philosophy
- Apparent enjoyment of position and accomplishment

Mentor

By contrast, in a facilitated mentoring process there is typically one *mentor* to one protégé, and each knows what is expected of the other. The mentor carries out some, or even all, of the functions of the sponsor and role model in a relationship structured around the skills that the protégé wants to develop or the experiences the protégé wishes to gain on an accelerated time schedule. In addition, a mentor may agree to perform one or more of these functions:

- Act as a source of information on the mission and goals of the organization
- Offer insight into the organization's philosophy of human resource development

- Tutor special skills, effective behavior, and how to function in the organization
- Give feedback on observed performances
- Coach activities that add to experience and skill development
- Serve as a confidant in times of personal crisis and problems
- Assist the protégé in plotting a career path
- Meet with the protégé at agreed time intervals for feedback and planning
- Agree to a no-fault conclusion of the mentoring relationship if (for any reason) the time is right
- Maintain the integrity of the relationship between the protégé and the natural boss or team leader

Such activities are clearly different from the more casual interactions that occur spontaneously with role models and sponsors. Strategies for avoiding duplication of effort or potential conflict with the line supervisor are discussed in the relevant chapters of Part Two.

Protégé

Popular labels for the *protégé* include *mentee, candidate, participant, apprentice, advisee, counselee, trainee,* and *student.* Less popular synonyms are *follower, subordinate, applicant, hopeful,* and *seeker.* Some organizations simply use the term *employee.* In a facilitated process, the candidate for protégé has, at a minimum, these characteristics:

- Willingness to assume responsibility for his or her own growth and development
- Assessed and self-perceived growth potential
- Ability to perform in more than one skill area
- A record of seeking challenging assignments and new responsibilities
- Receptivity to feedback and coaching

From here on in this book, the words *mentor* and *protégé* imply these characteristics and responsibilities unless otherwise noted. Part Two of this book gives additional insight into the factors that influence the choice of title for mentors and protégés in organizations.

This brief discussion has given a historical overview of mentoring and working definitions of the mentor and protégé roles. Chapter Two takes a closer look at the reasons for the increasing interest in facilitated mentoring in public and private organizations.

Chapter Two

Mentoring at Work in Organizations

A list of those who publicly acknowledge the value of their mentoring relationships resembles a Who's Who of the professions, business, sports, arts, and social activism. The comments here on the interaction of selected notable pairs illustrate the deep and continuing impact of mentoring relationships in many environments. Some of these pairings obviously just happened. Other connections were apparently initiated through work or professional proximity. In the past few years an increasing percentage of these relationships are planned, deliberate, *facilitated*, to support organization and individual participant goals and needs. Still, it is interesting that even when the mentor and protégé work in the same field, their backgrounds and work styles are often quite diverse.

Selected Examples of Mentoring Benefits

The specific quotes presented here were selected to illustrate the variety of benefits to one or both parties in a mentoring relationship.

Acting

Larry D. Clark, dean of arts and sciences at the University of Missouri, Columbia, was a mentor to Tom Berenger, the Academy Award–nominee actor. Berenger, who came to the University of Missouri as a journalism major, tried out for a play that Clark was directing. The relationship sparked, and Berenger changed his major to theater. Clark (interview by the author, 1990) says, "Tom soaked up technique so fast that it never seemed as if it was a mentor-protégé relationship. It was more like a mutual learning situation—all of us used his talent to refine our work. He made me realize fully how much the mentor can learn from the exceptional protégé." From the viewpoint of the protégé, Berenger (interview by the author, 1990) comments, "In the theater, you often learn without knowing where or how it happened. A good mentor helps you to know when you've got it right and, more importantly, helps you know how to do it again. I believe that holds true for all walks of life."

Banking

Good leaders always seek ways to further hone their skills. Paul Maltby, a manager in personal banking with the Royal Bank of Canada, says, "I'd like to improve, though. The best way to pick up the less tangible skills I need is to draw on the insights of people with years of experience." Mentor Rosanne Le Donne adds, "I've picked up insights into managing people from Paul" (Murray, 1999a).

Consulting

In the growing technical consulting field, there is intense competition for recruiting, developing, and retaining talented people. Tanaz Sowdagar of AGConsulting expresses her appreciation of her mentor's support: "Through my mentor I learned how to be proactive and get closer to my goals within my organization. By sharing my client stories with my mentor, I learned how to look at some issues and incidents from a different angle. She also supported me giving advice on how to approach the challenges I was facing at the time" (personal communication with the author, Apr. 14, 2000).

Golf

Earl Woods fills the double role of mentor and parent, passing on both professional and life skills and learning in the process. "I want to emphasize . . . this wasn't a 'training process' for Tiger [Woods, his protégé and son]; it was just an opportunity for me to give him something I had never given anybody else . . . my time, effort, and attention. I always encouraged Tiger to question what I was saying and, if he found me in error, to let me know so I could learn, too" (Woods, 1997).

Insurance

"Larry, my current mentor, seemed to be a natural match for me. He has technical experience in the discipline that I'm interested in, and his career path has been one to which I aspire." Allstate Insurance initially implemented the program to keep up with competitors, changing expectations, and to ensure "superior" returns to shareholders (Darling, 1997).

Nuclear Regulation

Cynthia Dekle, of the Nuclear Regulatory Commission, is lavish in her praise of mentor Beth De Woody's help with advanced information technology applications: "Once I got into the mentoring program, I became focused on how to use this new technology to my benefit" ("EEO Works," 2000, p. 1).

Power Utility

"Once Chuck [Ackerman] was added to the [first line supervisor succession] plan, he was offered the opportunity to participate in the pilot of the FENOC [First Energy Nuclear Operating Company]-facilitated mentoring process. He took this opportunity and was paired with Scott Coakley, work control manager. Together, they constructed a developmental plan to help Chuck focus on improving his performance in the ten competencies necessary to be a first-line supervisor" (D. Laberdee, e-mail to author, Feb. 16, 2000).

Social Activists

Benjamin E. Mays was mentor to Martin Luther King Jr. ("Obituary," 1984, p. B2). King was heard to say that he was "awakened both intellectually and spiritually by my mentor, Dr. Benjamin E. Mays."

Technology and E-Commerce

"In our division at Andersen [Consulting, now known as Accenture] we had a need to motivate our top performers to continue learning and stay at the top of their game in this fast-paced industry. We turned to mentoring to fulfill our need. We captured the knowledge of our most skilled employees through our protégés, protecting our knowledge capital—our biggest asset" (J. K. Ehlen, e-mail to author, Sept. 7, 2000).

The list could go on. Many people proclaim the positive influence of mentors on their lives—particularly people in business, and increasingly those in nonprofit organizations. An international management consulting firm, Heidrick and Struggles, surveyed 1,250 prominent men and women executives in the late 1970s (Roche, 1979) to determine the factors contributing to their success. Nearly two-thirds of those surveyed reported having had a mentor or sponsor. The positive results were measurable, and they had less tangible indicators as well. "Executives who have had a mentor earned more money at a younger age, . . . are happier with their progress, and derive greater pleasure from their work" (p. 15).

It is highly likely that the historical examples of mentoring relationships just happened through some spontaneous interaction of the two people. Either party may have initiated the contact. The protégé may have thought *I'd like to learn more from that person* or may have seen the person do something that had good results; success is seductive. Or the mentor may have been unconsciously attracted to the fresh perspective of the protégé and may have offered a few suggestions for furthering the protégé's work. No matter who initiated the first exchange, both parties undoubtedly felt good about the results of that interaction and sought additional contact. The seeds of a productive relationship were sown in fertile ground, while shared achievement continued to strengthen the bond.

Many of the relationships described in popular publications have been such happenstance occurrences. A sales manager in a furniture manufacturing firm expressed it this way: "I'm looking, but I'm keeping a low profile; if you're too open about it your search might backfire. It seems to me that searching for a mentor is a lot like looking for love: it has to sneak up on you if it's really going to be right" (Blotnick, 1984, p. 9). However, Blotnick's survey of twenty-five executives concluded that without some guidance there is "nothing surefire about . . . finding a suitable mentor" (p. 9). Articles (Robinson, 1990; Zuckerman, 1990) now indicate that the trend is toward putting some formal structure into the matching of mentor and protégé. The more recent examples in the previous section are all from facilitated processes in which the organization realized beneficial results, as well as the participants.

Motives for Facilitated Mentoring

What perceived needs are generating this increased interest in formalized mentoring? The program booklet for the International Society for Performance Improvement's 2000 conference asserts, "Organizations are under pressure to maintain a competitive edge by increasing efficiency, reducing costs, and improving performance." Filling the wisdom gaps created by accelerated growth and the job hopping of thirty-something professionals has strained the resources of many organizations. We talk lifelong learning, speak about creating learning organizations, and assign the title of chief learning officer, but we still have difficulty putting those learnings into a meaningful context for performance improvement in this chaotic business climate. These and additional phenomena may be motivating executives and administrators in both the public and private sectors to consider increasing the amount of structure in their mentoring processes.

Need for Leadership

Burt Nanus and Stephen Dobbs describe the common themes of leadership in the public and private sector arenas as purpose, hope, inspiration, influence, marshaling resources, and effecting change: "We offer our own definition: a leader of a nonprofit organization is a person who marshals the people, capital, and intellectual resources of the organization to move it in the right direction" (Nanus and Dobbs, 1999, p. 6).

Theory-Based Formal Education and Real-World Needs

My master's thesis for the School of Management at John F. Kennedy University was a study of the curricula of five business schools. I found that the offered courses addressed only half of the sixteen skills identified by my research as vital signs for mastery in management. Skills relevant to organizing and planning, quality of decisions, leadership, behavior flexibility, inner work standards, group process, technical job knowledge, and salesmanship and marketing were taught in one or more courses at each university. But none of the business schools offered courses with the stated objectives of developing students' skills in decisiveness, creativity, written communication, oral communication, tolerance of uncertainty, resistance to stress, energy, or use of personal power.

The results of the study confirmed the hypothesis that a significant gap exists between the skills required for successful management performance and the skills taught in a traditional business school. It would be naïve to suggest that any one business school curriculum will ever fulfill all needs for all students, although certainly the relevance of courses taught in most schools could be improved. However, four of the skills that are most often neglected in school curricula—decisiveness, tolerance of uncertainty, resistance to stress, and use of personal power—are particularly appropriate for modeling and coaching by a skillful mentor.

Functional Illiteracy of Entry-Level Employees

According to the National Institute for Literacy, graduates from secondary schools in the United States are entering the workforce unprepared to perform at a satisfactory level. Basic career and life skills such as reading and simple mathematics are inadequate: "At least 40 million adults in the U.S. need stronger literacy skills in order to take full advantage of continuing lifelong learning opportunities" ("Margins to the Mainstream," 2000). Companies are recognizing the long-term impact on their businesses of these skill deficiencies. CBS News reported in July 1989 that BellSouth, with its long-standing reputation for hiring people into entry-level jobs and promoting to supervisory, management, and executive levels from within, made a sizable contribution to special programs for improving basic skills training in secondary schools in their employment area. Even with such special programs, the deficiencies will not be eliminated overnight. Peer-group mentors in entry-level positions may be an effective resource to fill part of the gap.

Disenchantment with Traditional Training Programs

There is growing disenchantment with conventional educational and training programs offered within organizations. Most organizations offer a menu of generic management and supervisory training programs—for example, courses in time management and basic communication—as well as technical or job-specific courses. Such formal training for specific skills is essential, and we are not suggesting that it be replaced by mentoring. However, when training courses use traditional academic formats such as lecture and presentation, the busy manager gets frustrated and bored. Often the content of the course is aimed at the "average" person and an insult to an experienced professional. Many times there is no follow-up to determine whether skills are applied back on the job. All too often, bosses lack the motivation or ability to reinforce and build on skills learned by trainees in a course.

The bottom line is that attitudinal and behavioral changes are extremely difficult to accomplish, especially for the individual left on his or her own. In formal training the *content* may be conveyed but not the *context* for application of that knowledge to the work environment. The perceptions and experiences of the mentor provide that context, as well as a model of behavior worthy of emulation.

Expanding Awareness of Performance Technology

As organizations are downsized, they seek opportunities to increase the cost effectiveness of human resource development. Fortunately, at the same time they are becoming aware of the efficacy of performance technology. The strategies of performance technology can be applied to analyzing and designing a facilitated mentoring process that is targeted to fill the gap between the skill requirements for a function and its tasks on the one hand and the current skills of the job incumbent on the other. Performance technology also provides the strategies for evaluating the impact of the mentoring experience on the competence of the protégé and the results of the organization.

Need to Respond to Legal Action

Rarely is the term *affirmative action* used today, but even so there is a surge of interest in mentoring processes for women and minorities in the United States. Recent queries about our mentoring experiences have come from a spectrum of companies and organizations—aerospace, education, telecommunications, glass manufacturing, tobacco, grocery distribution, information technology, retail clothing, and accounting—all citing the need to develop women and members of underrepresented groups for management positions to meet equal opportunity goals. In a few cases, these organizations had been sued for discrimination against certain classes of workers. Some settlement agreements are now including a requirement to put a mentoring process in place. One example is the case brought by Dr. Margaret Jensvold, who charged that the National Institute of Mental Health sexually discriminated against her. She asserts that mentoring played a crucial part in her electing to take a job at NIH because she expected to progress in her field of study by working and learning from someone already established in the business area of her study. The Jensvold case is expected to establish that mentoring is covered under sex discrimination law (Corbin, 1994). This may not be the most desirable motivation, yet it is compelling to action.

Awareness of the Needs of a Diverse Workforce

Employees must pursue professional development and take personal responsibility for their own growth if they wish to maintain required skills. Because few people have the skills and objectivity to assess accurately their own developmental needs, employers must establish the environment and some of the resources that support this growth. The workforce of the twenty-first century is an entirely new one, as restructuring efforts shape incentives for early retirement and new employees are increasingly women and minorities. The *Annual Report Fiscal Year 1999* of the U.S. Department of Labor reports women now comprise 47 percent of America's 139 million workers. Further, the DOL projects that African Americans, Hispanics, Asians, and other minorities will account for about two-thirds of new workers between now and 2008 (U.S. Department of Labor, 1999). In addition, in the United States and some other countries, changes in welfare reform laws are bringing people into the workforce who may have no family history of work. Many of those newly hired have even less ability than current employees to accurately assess which of their skills are relevant to job requirements, particularly beyond an entry-level position.

A visual scan of any office or shop illustrates that diversity in the workforce is no longer a white-and-black issue. Supervisors in multicultural work environments find significant differences in workers who are American-born minorities and recent immigrants from those same ethnic groups. Generalizations about groups create trouble, especially in designing performance-improvement programs. Not all Asians respond to the same structure, any more than all Americans do. For example, workers from Taiwan do not share the strong team concept prevalent among Japanese workers. In Taiwan, competitiveness is often the norm. Our colleagues in Argentina, Brazil, Chile, and Mexico often remind me that they are Americans, too, with different cultural norms and work patterns from each other and from North Americans. Sensitivity to the differences of people and attention to individual needs and wants in the workplace is increasingly important and complex.

Need to Replace an Aging Workforce

The federal government will face a crisis of competence when fifty-seven thousand baby boomers hit the optional retirement age of fifty-five in the year 2002 (Carmichael, 1988). Most hiring in the public sector takes place at the clerical and administrative levels, and higher-level positions are filled by promotion from within. Procedures for moving up from the entry level to middle levels of administration have long been established. The mounting number of retirements will create a critical need for seasoned executives.

Two agencies, the General Accounting Office (GAO) and the Internal Revenue Service, are addressing this need by using a mentoring process to make the younger administrator ready for executive responsibility. From 1984 to 1989, fifty-five candidates for the senior executive service in the GAO participated in the Executive Candidate Development Program (ECDP), which has a mentoring element (Glazer and Murray, 1990). The ECDP is one component of the overall management-development plan. Individuals accepted into the ECDP are expected to develop the managerial competence required of leaders at the executive level within eighteen months.

The wisdom of capturing the accumulated knowledge—the intellectual capital of the organization—prior to the exit of that first wave of retirees is just beginning to hit the consciousness of many leaders. We are discussing a mentoring process for one organization that will retire 19 percent of its managers in five years and 43 percent total in less than ten years. Consciousness was raised by a systematic organization chart analysis, color coding key positions occupied by soon-to-be-retired persons.

Recognition of Increasing Labor-Management Cooperation

Training and development programs offered by unions are becoming increasingly comprehensive and sophisticated. Apprenticeship is a respected tradition in many crafts and industries. It is a logical progression from an apprentice-master relationship to a mentoring relationship designed to produce competence in high-technology jobs and in areas that are often described as soft and complex.

Labor and management are beginning to recognize that to prosper in a changing, increasingly competitive environment they must change the way they relate to one another. When I was a line manager in the 1960s and 1970s, the unions objected to managers' singling out any of their members for special training and resisted development plans designed for individuals (such as a mentoring relationship). Now there is growing appreciation among labor and management professionals that collaborative labor systems are more productive than adversarial ones: "Labor and management must be equipped with *partnership skills* so they can work together to develop a work environment that will meet the challenges of the year 2000 and beyond" (Dinnocenzo, 1988, p. 71).

Changes in Companies That Are Restructuring

Restructuring companies need strong, generalist managers who can make a successful transition from one industry or technical area to another. Also needed are managers who can move from a professional or technical specialty, such as engineering, to a totally different function, such as marketing manager. This need grows as

jobs in the service sector increase while jobs in the production sector decrease: "Service and white-collar occupations increasingly
dominate the work world, while export-related jobs in manufacturing reflect an America that has become increasingly intertwined
with the global economy" (U.S. Department of Labor, 1999, p. 6).

Volatility in functions within organizations cause people to
change career fields many times. One placement firm estimates that
many employees will have seven or more entirely different job
functions in their career experience. Older, more experienced
workers have to learn new skills—and learn them from younger
supervisors, mentors, or peers.

Employers are now recognizing that early retirement is drain-
ing their intellectual capital. Passing on this investment in the
knowledge and skills of the retiring person to the successor is smart
management of assets.

Need for Succession Planning and Management Development

With the fast growth of service and knowledge organizations, society is becoming increasingly dependent on what Sveiby and Lloyd
call *knowhow* (1987, p. 18): "Knowhow companies solve complex,
nonstandardized problems; traditional service companies solve simple ones." Examples of traditional service companies are banks,
fast-food restaurants, and machinery repair shops. Knowhow companies are those that provide services totally adapted to the client,
such as law firms, portfolio managers, and telecommunications
design companies.

Succession planning becomes increasingly important in service
and knowledge-based organizations. The most skilled professional
or technical person may be the poorest candidate for manager. The
skills required to troubleshoot an equipment malfunction or sell a
product are quite different from those needed to manage a group of
professional engineers or salespeople. The technical person's desire
to "do it better than those guys can" gets in the way of managing

and leading the effort. However, selection of top management from outside an organization still is the exception rather than the rule. Most top people grow and develop in an up-through-the-ranks process. Therefore, implementation of a succession planning program is critical; again, Sveiby and Lloyd say that "if it is to survive long-term, the professional organization must develop enough competent 'seniors' to discharge the responsibilities of top management" (1987, p. 110).

Movement Toward Facilitated Mentoring

Whatever the stimulus, the interest in careful planning of the mentoring process is growing all over the world. Here is a selected list of the types of organizations that have some form of structured mentoring process:

- Industry
- Government
- Nonprofit
- Community-based
- Youth
- Foundations
- Education

A partial list of companies and organizations mentioned in various publications and presentations includes Allstate Insurance, Ameritech, Andersen Consulting Technical Services, Apple Computer, Arnott's Biscuit Manufacturers, AT&T, Australian Red Cross Blood Services, Dow Jones, DuPont, California Women in Government, Chevron Information Technology Company, Chubb and Son, Federal Express, Finland Civil Service, First Energy, the General Accounting Office, General Motors, Glendale Federal Savings, Hewlett-Packard, Hughes Aircraft, IBM, the Internal Revenue Service, Jewel Tea, Lockheed Martin, Lucent IT Poland,

Merrill Lynch, New York University, the Nuclear Regulatory Commission, Royal Bank of Canada, Sandia Laboratories, Shell Oil Services, Starwood Hotels and Resorts in Latin America, Sun Microsystems, and Teradyne South Asia.

One international survey (PA Personnel Services, 1986) conducted in the 1980s in eight countries found sixty-seven organizations (18 percent of those surveyed) with formal (their term) mentoring programs. The majority of organizations that had implemented these programs reported that they were pleased with the results of the mentoring efforts. A survey by *Human Resource Executive* magazine in 1996 produced the startling finding that the percentage of businesses planning mentoring programs doubled in one year, to 36 percent (Jossi, 1997). Some of the organizations just named show a worldwide increasing interest in facilitated mentoring. My colleagues and I are working with facilitated mentoring processes in sixteen countries now, with both national companies and multinational ones.

Setting up a mentoring process specifically designed to benefit the organization has now become a priority. Aggressive competition for talent and the costs of replacing key people who leave have made recruitment and retention of employees a business imperative. Development for future career positions was previously largely limited to top executives and often given as a reward rather than because of an assessed need. Typically, the training for other employees was directed at current job skills. Now mentoring processes are being instituted with the explicit goal of increasing company profitability by making individuals more productive. Other companies—feeling the direct financial impact of being fined for not complying with affirmative-action agreements—are investigating ways to establish mentoring processes specifically for women and minorities. When we ask clients why they want to implement a mentoring process, we hear these responses (Murray, 1995):

- To make sure we are retaining the right people as we "rightsize"
- To attract and recruit people with the requisite skills for tomorrow's demands

- To make our experienced and skilled people feel valued
- To increase the likelihood that we will survive
- To improve results—profit or otherwise—with people who are more competent, confident, experienced, and motivated
- To ensure representation of diverse groups in all levels of the organization
- To enable our people to learn to work with others with different educations, ages, cultures, physical abilities, etc.
- To improve communication across functional or divisional lines

A survey of 636 mentor-protégé pairs revealed that 42 percent had been matched for career development of the protégé, 30 percent were targeting technical skills transfer, and 12 percent had been paired in support of cross-functional and cultural diversity (Murray, 1999b).

Many organizations that have implemented mentoring processes do not have ways to measure the direct impact of the process on productivity or individual performance. One might think that the need for evaluating is obvious. If there is a costly gap in capability that must be filled, astute managers want to know the cost of the solution and whether the solution really works. However, costly programs of all sorts have been put in place because a manager or administrator wanted it, not because of an assessed need. Rarely is the evaluation and tracking mechanism designed into the process itself. More often, an evaluation is done only after someone questions the costs. Strategies for evaluating a facilitated mentoring process are suggested in Chapter Thirteen.

Also, deliberately pairing mentors with protégés in a facilitated process may not be acceptable in some organizational cultures. For example, having an employee paired with someone other than his or her line boss might be seen as disloyal or subversive behavior. This is not to suggest that any one culture is right or wrong. Criticism of a culture as being wrong may stimulate a strong defense of the status quo. It is then even more difficult to bring about the desired changes. An organization's culture evolves over the years and may continue for decades, even though the people who helped to shape it are no longer there. Cultural change is a slow process in most environments, and structuring a mentoring process as the sole agent of such change is likely to fail.

Structured or facilitated mentoring is thus not for everyone. It is also not the magic potion for solving all organizational ills. Some organizations look to mentoring as a way to avoid the formidable task of developing unskilled managers and supervisors. This solution is shortsighted at best and can create monstrous problems because one then has to work around the managers who lack basic people skills. A mentoring process should be one component of a comprehensive system of people development. For sustained effectiveness, it must be carefully integrated with the other components of that system: training programs, performance appraisals, and recruitment. When all managers and supervisors have the skills and strengths to assist their associates with career planning, skill development, and growth, the need for a special mentoring process may diminish. However, even then mentors can continue to impart added value by helping prepare people for different functional responsibilities.

Do these current trends, examples, and motives make you think that facilitated mentoring may be worth investigating for your organization? Chapters Three, Four, and Five illustrate the benefits and issues of a mentoring process for the organization, the protégé, and the mentor. Chapter Seven presents strategies to help you assess your organization's readiness for a facilitated mentoring process. The specific guidelines given there help you design your process to realize the full benefits of the mentoring process and avoid many problems.

Chapter Three

The Upside and the Downside for the Organization

Major multinational corporations are implementing facilitated mentoring processes to support priority goals of growth, profit, market share, and return to shareholders. One organization lamented that its staffing of due diligence teams for assessment of potential business acquisitions had stripped the line management ranks of experienced people. With its limited product line, growth in this organization can only be attained by buying businesses in other geographical locations. The larger overall organization allows economy of scale with standard technology for distribution, financial procedures, and human resources. The outcome sought from the mentoring process was to speed development of strong line managers to maintain the success of the core business.

Nonprofit groups are also seeking the benefits of the mentoring process to support necessary, rapid staff development and retention. When the talent pool is shallow, foundations and nonprofits cannot compete with salaries offered by profitable businesses. Shortening the learning curve to make new staff members and volunteers competent and productive fundraisers is an attractive outcome of the mentoring process for these small offices: "Volunteers teach one another new skills and techniques, and trade knowledge. Networking with colleagues at other non-profits expands the potential to find needed mentors" ("Inexpensive MD-Nonprofits," 1992, p. 4).

A pilot launched by the U.S. Small Business Administration's Office of Women's Business Ownership to pair experienced female CEOs with entrepreneurial women in business for a time period less than one year "found that growth occurred in the protégés' businesses. This was reflected in increased receivables, number of customer/client prospects, number of employees, and number of accounts" (Small Business Administration, 1990, p. 11).

Research in Australia found mentoring to be viewed as an important management tool: "Formal or institutionalized mentorship goes one step further by making mentorship a systemic policy issue and a standard part of management practice" (Ehrich and Hansford, 1999, p. 95).

Examples of the successes and difficulties with mentoring in industry, government, health care, nonprofit organizations, and education are cited throughout this and the remaining chapters. These examples eloquently attest to the fact that any organization—be it a large corporation or a small volunteer agency—must be aware of the positive and negative aspects of facilitated mentoring. It must be able to weigh the pros and cons and be willing to take the risks. Otherwise, such a program will never get off the ground, and if it does, it will likely be short-lived.

Benefits to the Organization

On the upside for the organization, consider these positive points of facilitated mentoring.

Increased Productivity

"Multiskilled, flexible people add greater value to down-sized leaner, flatter organizations" (Murray, 1998, p. 37). Hard work generally means increased productivity. When protégés adopt this ethic from their mentors, you can tally a plus for facilitated mentoring.

Mentor-protégé relationships can also give a boost to productivity through performance planning and increased teamwork. Tegwin Pulley, at Texas Instruments, reported that mentoring influences productivity: "The big advantage is mentoring helps employees contribute faster. They understand how to get things done in the system" (Tyler, 1998, p. 100). In the ideal facilitated mentoring process, the mentor, the protégé, and the protégé's manager or team leader plan projects and set standards for the protégé's performance. This teamwork approach, along with clear, measurable objectives for the protégé's performance, typically increases the protégé's motivation and leads to superior performance and high productivity.

Cost Effectiveness

One of the major benefits of the facilitated mentoring process is that it is cost-effective. In most processes, mentors carry out coaching responsibilities in addition to their regular job duties. (As Chapter Five makes clear, although mentoring often becomes just another part of the job it is important to build in financial or other types of reward for the mentor.) Similarly, protégés are expected to keep up individual job performance while participating in the mentor process, although most organizations allow some flexibility in scheduling and workload so that the protégé can meet with the mentor and complete related projects. In good processes, the protégé's development activities are targeted to the person's specific needs. The protégé thus gets highly relevant practice of needed skills without the cost of classroom training. With facilitated mentoring, there is no need to rent a room, no trainer to hire, and no excessive time off the job to compensate for. Unfortunately, many organizations do not have good data on the costs of formal training, making comparison of costs impossible.

We designed a process for the credit card service representatives in a bank that resulted in reducing the training time from twenty days for all new hires to an average of fourteen days. The 25 percent savings was attributed to a learning process that included modules for individual study and frequent coaching and feedback with a mentor. Mentor, a program developed within one of the Big Three automakers in Warren, Michigan, has succeeded in reducing the training orientation for novice engineering analysts by 87 percent. The learning methodology, called "just what's needed, just in time," assisted in creating the program, which "brings trainees to a required proficiency level in just three-and-a-half months. Prior to the division's use of 'Mentor,' it took up to two years to bring trainees up to speed" (Prism Performance Systems, 1994, p. 8).

Improved Recruitment Efforts

General Electric's Power Generation Division found mentoring to be a good training tool with an added plus. According to Louise O'Reilly (1989), manager of technical training, "We've also discovered that mentoring is a powerful concept in recruiting. Recognizing that the people we hire will be the future leaders of our company, we try to find the best students, develop them technically, and then continue to invest in them. Our college-campus interviewers impress upon the recruits that we just don't throw them into a difficult job and say good luck" (p. 4). A recruitment manager in a Canadian manufacturing business told us he had interviewed more than one hundred M.B.A. graduates as candidates for management positions. He was intrigued by the frequency of the question "Do you have a mentoring program?" and said he tallied eighty-seven interviewees asking this of him (interview with author, 1996). Many of these graduates had experienced a mentoring relationship in college and wanted to work in an organization that would support their continued growth.

This benefit holds true for educational organizations as well. In its mentoring program, Trinity College in Washington, D.C., brings together student mentees (protégés) and accomplished alumni mentors who coach them in selected skills and experiences in preparation for their chosen careers. In a survey conducted by Kirby (1989) all the respondents saw that the program "is good for the college; it shows that Trinity works." The program is a great success according to Mary Hayes, the committee chair: "There is overwhelming interest by both potential mentors and students to keep the program going" (interview by the author, 1990). At the secondary education level, Holy Names High School in Oakland,

California, creates mentoring relationships designed for HNHS juniors. Cynthia Wasko, college counselor and mentor administrator, explains, "HNHS is serious about women's education. That commitment must extend beyond the high school years. It must stretch farther than the stereotypical format of preparing young women for a 'cultured' life and become one of preparing them for business, learning what networking is and how to use it" ("Womanly Advice," 1994, p. 1).

Mentoring can also be used to recruit new employees into fields that are not currently popular. For example, though the retail business was not considered as attractive a career option as banking or the legal profession, Jewel Tea used mentoring as a magnet. In the words of Franklin J. Lunding, former chairman and chief executive officer, "We had to figure out ways of getting brains into the business. That's another way the 'first assistant' [a term they use for the mentor] philosophy helps the business; it attracts the smart ones" (Collins and Scott, 1978, p. 217).

More recently the U.S. government's School to Work initiative prompted General Motors to support its dealers in attracting high school students into automotive service technician jobs. Neither parents nor school counselors were recommending this job to students, due to the old stereotype that it was dirty and technicians did not have a very good reputation. The GMYES program matched students with master technicians and revealed to both students and parents that the complexity of today's automobiles makes this job require more of one's head than one's hands (Garcia and McCrary, 1997).

Facilitated mentoring processes can thus make organizations appealing to potential employees, students, or affiliates. The formal mentoring program at SC Johnson Wax is one reason why *Working Mother* magazine named it "one of the best companies to work for." The structured program pairs new employees with employees already established within the company ("Formal Mentoring Program," 1996).

The first few days in any type of organization—whether it is a business, school, professional group, or volunteer agency—can be stressful. The stress is lessened if a mentor is there to guide the protégé through the unfamiliar maze. The anxious new employee can be reassured by the image the mentoring process conveys of a solid organization that takes care of its members. There is an impact on productivity as well: "New hires are expected to be integrated into the company more quickly. . . . The mentoring process can facilitate that goal by reducing the learning curve so a new hire is producing results faster" (Dolainski, 2000).

Increased Organizational Communication and Understanding

The New York State Department of Taxation and Finance has offered cross-divisional mentoring to protégés since 1980. If the match is right, protégés can have mentors in offices across the state and in functional divisions different from their own. Mary Helen Rosenstein, director of staff development and training, says that one of the real benefits of facilitated mentoring to her organization is that people in the districts get a perspective on how the central office in Albany operates. "Sometimes when the central office makes a decision, it may not make sense to people out in the district offices," says Rosenstein (interview by the author, 1990). "There are times when people in the district offices complain, 'Hey, Albany doesn't know what's happening here.' But a protégé from a district office who has a mentor in Albany begins to see that the central office has to make decisions based on many factors: the legislature's actions, requests from the governor's office, the needs of other divisions in the department, and so on. The protégé takes that information back to the district office. So the program has been a very good communication vehicle."

Retaining Intellectual Capital and Maintaining Motivation

Long-time employees, no matter how dedicated and loyal, sometimes lose their zeal for the job. Doing the same thing year after year—no matter how well it is done—is not a challenge. Senior people who participate as mentors can rethink their philosophies and methods, benefit from the fresh ideas of protégés, and see their own styles emulated in the organization. Stuart, director of the Processing and Revenue Management Division of the same Department of Taxation and Finance and a mentor for ten years, expresses it this way: "Why do I do it? I suppose self-satisfaction that I can do something for other people who will eventually succeed me. It's nice to know that there are people in the organization who think you can do something for their career and further their understanding; if they think that I can be of some assistance, I'm pleased to do that" (interview by the author, 1990).

Kenneth Ehlen described the knowledge of the most skilled employees as Andersen Consulting's "knowledge capital—our biggest asset!" (e-mail to author, Sept. 7, 2000).

A mentoring program designed within DuPont works effectively to "preserve institutional memory and intellectual capital" (Jossi, 1997). At least once a month staff members and managers meet outside of supervision to discuss work-related issues; this enables the experienced managers to pass on their accumulated knowledge to others.

Enhancement of Services Offered by the Organization

It's no secret that human service agencies in the United States and many countries are facing a growing number of people in need. At the same time, the financial resources of many government and non-profit agencies are shrinking. Facilitated mentoring is fast becoming a way to strengthen and enhance human service agencies. Pilot programs in San Antonio, Texas; Marshall, Missouri; and Stamford, Connecticut, are pairing community mentors with women on welfare to help them make the transition into the world of work. The YWCA's Project Redirection—a teenage pregnancy-prevention program—matches community women with teens who need emotional support and coaching on parenting skills. In such instances, facilitated mentoring is a win-win situation: the organization's goals are furthered, clients get one-on-one assistance, caseworkers at the agencies can concentrate on managing and directing resources to the client, and mentors get a chance to be personally involved and make a positive difference in the lives of others.

Improvement in Strategic and Succession Planning

Typical long-range strategies for an organization are plans for market or operational areas, physical facilities, funding, and perhaps profits. Often they include staff projections based on anticipated growth and expected attrition. But these projections rarely include definite methods for recruiting, training, or promoting staff, even though these considerations could easily make or break a growing organization. Many organizations assume that they will be able to hire or promote well-qualified people during periods of growth, that perfect employees appear to fill vacant positions and perform up to speed in no time at all. Training and development programs, particularly for managers or administrators at higher levels, are often given the lowest priority. Only when the performance of a group of employees is not meeting the expectations of top management do decision makers give serious attention to human resource development in their strategic planning.

An organization with an effective mentoring process, however, can enhance strategic planning by having a concrete way to move people into higher-level jobs. Improved succession planning and management development was one of the benefits of a formalized mentoring program cited by 42 percent of the respondents to a study carried out by PA Personnel Services (1986).

Such systematic succession planning is critical. When the planners in an organization make their people projections, they often find that many seasoned managers will be retiring in a few years. To shorten the typical development cycle of future leaders, they often consider a mentoring program. This concern sparked the mentoring program at Federal Express (Crosby, 1987). An officer in the Maintenance and Engineering Division became interested in developing successors within his division. He identified mentoring as a natural component of succession planning. Mentoring then became a career-development tool for management preceptors (protégés) in Federal Express's Leadership Institute.

Challenges for the Organization

In Chapter Two I mentioned that facilitated mentoring is not for everyone. It has limitations and risks, just as all innovative programs do. Here are some of the negative, or downside, aspects of facilitated mentoring that organizations must consider.

Frustration

When there are few opportunities to move up in a leaner, flatter organization, a facilitated mentoring process designed to support succession planning may not be a wise investment. People with high aspirations who see limited opportunity to advance are not likely to listen to a litany of the other benefits of facilitated mentoring. In fact, instituting a mentoring process may add to the frustration of ambitious managers who know there is little opportunity to advance and who see investment in this special process as a misuse of scarce resources.

Commitment

The success of facilitated mentoring processes depends on the organization's strong commitment to developing and promoting people from within. Organizations where this philosophy is not clearly evident probably should not consider facilitated mentoring. To some protégés, the implicit promise of mentoring is upward mobility in the organization. It is essential to communicate clearly to all employees why the organization is implementing the mentoring process. We suggest it be stated that there are no guarantees of promotion or different assignments. One company president said this superbly: "I cannot guarantee you employment. I can assure you that the mentoring process will increase your employability" (conversation with the author, Jan. 5, 1999). If there are few opportunities for promotion, an organization cannot afford to make mistakes in filling vacancies. The appointed person must be well prepared for the position with all the skills and competencies to enable success.

Commitment to people, and to the mentoring process, is tested in other ways as well. From time to time, a protégé decides—as a result of close-up examination of values and developmental needs—to leave the company. This situation truly tests the commitment of the mentor and of the organization to people development: "A very talented individual has gone as far as he can in our company," explains Crosby. "He is being groomed to someday take over a small corporation outside of our company. He and his mentor discuss global issues not directly related to internal company matters" (1984, p. 2). This person continues to make a valued contribution to the company while he is there.

Financial and time commitments are further considerations. A mentoring process proves its efficacy in about three years. It takes time to iron out the wrinkles, integrate it with other human resource strategies, and evaluate its effectiveness. It is unrealistic to expect to see results of any substantive development program in less than one year. It takes several months to get the structure in place and the mentor-protégé relationships established and running smoothly. In addition, time and money for tracking and evaluating the results with mentors, with protégés, and for the organization are necessary. The evaluation process must generate data for continuous quality improvement as well as impact on the results of the organization. Anecdotal data on growth and satisfaction with the mentoring experience are reported in three or four months. Actual skill gains can sometimes be measured quickly, although visible improvement in generic management and leadership skills may take several months. Our experience shows it takes two to three years to make the mentoring process an integrated component of the culture.

The lack of true commitment to human resource development is an overwhelming obstacle to the success of any training effort. Without strong support from the top decision makers, a mentoring process will not survive its first budget review. The cost of any new initiative is always obvious, and the costs of not having it may be hidden.

Coordination with Other Performance Improvement Strategies

A mentoring process typically supports or supplements other people development programs in an organization. In the New York State Department of Taxation and Finance, protégés can also take advantage of an internal public administration training program. A company or agency with a large training department usually finds that mentoring strengthens existing programs by bridging the gap between classroom learning and real-world application. However, a lean organization, one that experiences many peak-and-valley workloads, probably does not have a large internal training and development department. Such an organization may find it cost-effective to use consultants as performance coaches.

Another caution is for organizations establishing facilitated mentoring as a separate, special program. Human resource people are often (and understandably) jealous of their areas of responsibility for training and development programs. Objections to mentoring as a new or special program that "won't work here" may really be a symptom of turf protection. The key is to have all concerned participate in the planning process and to integrate the mentoring component with all the other components of human resource development.

Hard to Sell

The lack of data on structured mentoring processes leads many decision makers to conclude that a formal process cannot be justified. There are few comprehensive studies of facilitated processes, probably because organizations do not take the time to analyze the results and publish reports of successful experiences. Also, it is difficult to isolate all the variables in order to make a direct correlation between a protégé's career success and mentoring. Because protégés typically seek out challenges and are ambitious and eager for self-improvement, determining whether they would have succeeded just as well without mentoring is a complicated task. In most cases, the best evidence that mentoring works is the praise of mentors and protégés who say that the mentoring experience was a benefit to both the organization and themselves.

In addition, mentoring can be difficult to describe to decision makers in an organization. Confusion about the roles and activities of mentors and protégés gives some cause for concern about the potential value of the mentoring process. It is sometimes much easier to talk about the magic or mystery of the experience than it is to describe exactly what takes place in the exchange. When the skills being taught to protégés are those of the crafts or trades, it is easy to describe the outcomes and to determine the investment for the organization. But when they are in management or administration, it is often difficult to measure the results and describe the mentor-protégé exchange. For example, one executive mentor explained that he simply let his protégés "get into my in-basket and see what's going on." Chapters Eight through Eleven give some useful descriptions of the roles and responsibilities of each person involved in a facilitated mentoring process.

Complicated and Expensive Administration

Cross-functional pairing requires extra coordination as well as equal commitment to mentoring from the leaders of both departments. Geographical distances may produce other complications and expense because most interactions are by e-mail, phone, or fax, or they involve travel. Time away from the job may make mentoring across functional areas too difficult to manage in some organizations. With advanced information technology and telecommunications, it is getting easier for mentoring pairs to successfully communicate even when geographically distant. Cross-functional pairing has been a clear benefit to many organizations in broadening the viewpoint of all the people involved. There are two key factors in reducing the costs of administration. One is the degree of responsibility taken by the protégé for assessing development needs and finding an appropriate potential mentor. The second is the ease of use of information databases of mentor profiles, skills templates, and development action plans. These subjects are discussed in greater depth in Chapters Eight, on the mentor role, and Nine, on protégé development planning.

We have mentioned here only some of the benefits and risks for an organization considering facilitated mentoring. As you weigh the pros and cons, keep in mind the attributes of your organization: goals, size, growth, human resource programs, top-level attitudes, financial status. Chapter Seven describes how to determine the readiness of your organization and how to make your decision about the worth of facilitating mentoring there.

Chapter Four

Payoffs and Penalties for the Protégé

Traditionally, those at the top of an organization have assumed the responsibility for planning the career path of an employee. Someone "up there" decides when to train, when to reassign, and when to promote employees at all levels. In many accounting firms, for example, the junior auditor is moved to auditor to senior auditor to manager to partner. It is assumed that the employee will go up or go out. In one organization in which I worked, there was a secret "ready now" binder that included profiles on managers who were targeted for movement in the company. (Often the first clue one had of being in the binder was a request to have a professional photograph taken.)

This ready-made career ladder can appeal to an employee, but in many such cases career goal setting follows the assignment rather than preceding it. Employees who accept this approach often feel that someone is playing puppeteer with the strings of their lives, yanking them this way and that to fit the current needs of the organization. The result can be apathy, dependency, frustration, stress, job burnout, and the loss of independent-minded employees who would prefer to integrate their own values and ambitions with those of the organization—truly a high price.

What can facilitated mentoring do to aid these valuable employees who feel stuck? First, facilitated mentoring creates a pathway for those who want to "walk to meet their luck." In such a process, protégés serve their own interests by participating in setting goals and creating action plans to attain them. Quite often this activity pays off in tangible ways. Carol Kleiman conducted a study

47

(1991) that proves women with mentors move more quickly up the corporate ladder and in general receive more promotions throughout their careers.

Second, a mentor can direct people to positions in the organization that match their interests and skills. In such cases, a skillful mentor can save the organization costly turnover.

Third, caring and informed mentors can help people avoid careers that are unsuitable. Educational mentoring programs can keep youths out of jobs that are inappropriate and that would lead to failure. In an interesting twist, many college students in teacher training programs are offered the option of becoming mentors for high school youth. If these teacher candidates (protégés) are unable to demonstrate promise as mentors, they are then advised by their own mentors to find suitable careers! In industry, employees are sometimes counseled by their mentors to eventually leave the company. One such situation is described by Crosby as benefiting everyone involved, even the company: "We realize we can't offer him everything, but in the meanwhile, during the three to five years the process takes, the company is benefiting from his productivity and enthusiasm" (1984, p. 2).

One organization reported more than $8,000 in savings because one hour with a mentor enabled an applicant to see she did not want a particular job. The training for that position was extensive and expensive, and they avoided the projected costs of the course.

Benefits for the Protégé

Here are the most common benefits to protégés cited in the literature and in our experience with facilitated mentoring processes, with a brief selected example of each:

• *Making the school-to-career transition.* In the AYES program (D. I. Gray, e-mail to author, Sept. 7, 2000), the student intern develops automotive repair skills learning from both the classroom instructor and the master service technician mentor in the dealership. The mentor validates those skills when they are demonstrated at the worksite by stamping the intern's "passport." This program prepares the student intern to continue postsecondary study leading to industry certification.

- *Rapid assimilation into the culture.* A program at Ameritech (a telecommunications company) pairs new hires with experienced employees in order to help "newcomers ease into the company without squelching the ideas, attitudes or skills for which they were hired in the first place" (Gunn, 1995).

- *Accelerated leadership development.* Hewlett-Packard uses strategies of personnel technology to achieve success with a twelve-month accelerated development program for high potential employees (Laabs, 1993).

- *Higher earnings.* Kathryn Tyler reports that professionals who have had mentors earn between $5,610 and $22,450 more annually than those who have not (Tyler, 1998). Betsy Cash Woolfolk, a twelve-year Million Dollar Round Table member in the insurance industry, has tripled her production rate over the past five years through mentoring (Million Dollar Round Table, 1994).

- *Advancement of underrepresented groups.* For example, the number of minority persons in top management positions at DuPont has risen 10 to 35 percent since mentoring was first implemented within the company in 1985 (Granfield, 1992).

- *Shorter learning curve with technical skills.* The changing marketplace and effects of a global economy demand the more rapid acquisition of skills. This is especially critical with rapidly changing technology (Duncan, 1995).

- *Increased job satisfaction.* This is important on the part of *all* participants (J. K. Ehlen, e-mail to author, Sept. 7, 2000).

- *Value added to education.* A study conducted by Catalyst found that within the Fortune 1,000 companies, 81 percent of women executives had mentors and valued them above their educational credentials (Touby, 1998).

- *Greater influence in the organization.* Ashley Fields, lead coordinator for Shell Oil Company's mentoring process, stated, "Our hope is that participants will look back on this mentoring relationship and realize it was one of the most beneficial experiences of their careers in terms of moving to the next level of impact in an organization" ("Mentoring Mentees," 2000, p. 13).

Here is a closer look at some striking payoffs for protégés who participate in facilitated mentoring processes.

• *Targeted development activities.* What typically happens when a person's skill deficiencies surface through self-perception, a supervisor's appraisal, or some other form of assessment? Quite often a training course or seminar is found or designed to fill the person's needs. Such courses may or may not give the person the exact skills, knowledge, and practice needed to become a good performer.

In good facilitated mentoring processes, however, interested parties produce a development plan that addresses the exact needs of the protégé. In most businesses, this development plan is formulated by the protégé, the mentor, the protégé's natural boss, and the process coordinator, who identify specific ways to develop the protégé's skills. Not only are they likely to match training or practice to the need, but accountability is built into the process by having all four parties agree on the processes to be pursued.

Wells Fargo Bank used this skills-based approach when it developed its Branch Manager MAP (meaning, a guide; MAP is not an acronym) program. Skills needed to perform branch manager functions were identified, and activities were then selected that would promote developing those skills. For example, the branch manager can be required to read policies and answer questions, talk with model bank employees, or complete a self-study course in communication. As part of the program, each branch manager is also assigned a MAP manager—a higher-level executive who can waive or add to these developmental activities according to the employee's needs and performance—who functions as a mentor. The MAP manager gives support and direction to the branch manager, providing key information on the culture and inner workings of the organization that could never be gained in a general training class (Roger Addison, interview by the author, 1989).

• *Increased likelihood of success*. Charlie Hartness, a popular and valued mentor (now retired) among the managers at Federal Express, comments: "Simply avoiding failure is not all that it takes to be successful. I think probably the most important contribution a mentor can make to candidates is helping them to avoid failure. They will succeed on the basis of their own competencies, as long as they avoid failing in the process" (quoted in Avant and Crosby De Berry, 1985).

This philosophy that fewer failures increases the likelihood of success is causing mentoring to become an important educational tool, particularly for at-risk youth. At the 1990 National Mentoring Conference, presentations were made on using mentoring to maximize the expertise of mentor teachers and to increase the retention rate of blacks and other minority students. Project Literacy U.S. (PLUS) is engineering a mentoring project called One PLUS One. Its goal is to promote formal mentoring to further literacy, academic achievement, career goals, and self-esteem in young people. Lauro F. Cavazos, U.S. secretary of education, states:

> The risks that all young people face are compounded for those who are poor, members of racial or ethnic minorities, or recent immigrants. These youths often attend the weakest schools, have fewer successful adult role models, . . . and have the fewest clearly visible paths to opportunities in the mainstream. For these youngsters, studies are finding that those who receive support from a mature, caring adult—a mentor—are more likely to finish high school and more likely to hold a job. These are significant behavior changes, and necessary ones, because we as a society cannot afford to allow our children to fail. Their failures are not only personal tragedies but also direct threats to our national standard of living and our democratic institutions [1990, p. 1].

A mentor can literally make the difference between keeping and losing a hard-won job for the new employee coming off the welfare rolls and obtaining employment for the first time. Nationwide in the United States, people from second- and third-generation family welfare recipients are forced to seek jobs when welfare benefit limits have expired. The new employees may have little or no experience with work rules and ethics. Handling issues with child care, transportation, and getting to work on time are overwhelming challenges to some of them. A caring mentor who can work across differences of age, work experience, and values can help the new hire bridge this career change chasm.

• *Less time spent in the wrong position.* "I'm bored. My skills aren't being used. I feel like I have nowhere to go. I'm tracked into a career path I didn't want to be in. The only way for me to make more money is to move into management, but I don't want to be a manager." So goes the lament of employees who are not able to match their interests with the organization's needs. They spend their workdays in misery and dissatisfaction until they quit, feeling that they have wasted their time in a career or organization they didn't care about.

• *The Pygmalion effect.* Dione Gomez was lazy and she knew it. That's why she asked George Curry, New York bureau chief for the *Chicago Tribune,* to be her mentor. When Gomez began procrastinating about writing news stories, Curry wrote what he described as a blistering letter. "Basically I told her to put up or shut up," Curry said in his endearing way (interview by the author, 1990). Gomez is more complimentary. "Basically, George said he thought I had potential. He told me 'I think you can do well. I have faith in you. I think you have potential, and I think you can get it together.' And I did. Now he introduces me to his colleagues as his first mentee in New York. He's proud of me, and it feels great" (interview by the author, 1990). Gomez has since had several front-page stories in publications, and she plans one day to have a job much like Curry's.

This story illustrates an interesting payoff for protégés. Bosses, teachers, even parents often expect people to perform just the way they have all along. But a mentor has fewer biases about what someone has done in the past and tends to see potential that no one else does. The mentor can create the expectation that the protégé will do more and do it better than before. Just like Eliza Doolittle with the tutoring of Professor Higgins, the protégé achieves well because both parties expect it. A powerful mentor also reflects power on a protégé. The visibility of the relationship sends a signal to others that the protégé has access to the resources and power of the mentor.

- *Increased awareness of the organization.* When the protégé has a mentor at a higher level in the organization, important information is passed on in their discussions. This communication is likely to be more effective, and certainly more timely, than company newsletters or management bulletins. The protégé who knows the future direction of the organization can design career plans accordingly and can focus development activities on the changing requirements of the business. For example, when companies converted mechanical and electrical equipment and devices to electronic ones, many engineers found their skills obsolete. Had they known ahead of time about this shift in direction, those who were motivated to stay with a company could have pursued training in electronics.

Awareness of other industries, professions, or careers is a potential benefit when a mentor is outside the protégé's current organization. These different-organization relationships are not often designed as a facilitated mentoring process, yet many people have described to us great value accruing to them from such a relationship.

Possible Pitfalls for the Protégé

The mentoring relationship does not always work out in the protégé's favor. Sometimes it can lead to problems and frustrating experiences. Here are some potential pitfalls to consider.

Expectation That the Protégé Will Neglect the Core Job

Let's face it. Some managers and supervisors are convinced that their direct reports are out to cheat the company. For example, many supervisors continue to resist flextime work schedules and

teleworking, although studies show they result in increased productivity and job satisfaction. Apparently this resistance is an indi-
cator of their concern that people do not work without close
supervision. It is fairly common to hear managers express the concern that development activities suggested by the mentor are so
attractive and engrossing that the employee will neglect the routine job. Undoubtedly, a protégé who is not ready for self-management sometimes slips through the most careful screening process.
But there is overwhelming evidence that such a person is the
exception to the rule. When people feel that intelligent consideration is given to their growth and development, they often exert
great effort to perform in all aspects of the job.

Expectation That the Protégé Will Play Mentor Against the Boss

True, if the relationship between the boss and the associates is not
a good one, the protégé reaches out to the mentor for positive
interaction. This is a good reason to include the boss as well as the
mentor in development planning. Such an arrangement helps
diminish subversive behavior and makes the roles and responsibilities of everyone involved in the mentoring relationship crystal
clear. Chapters Eight, Nine, and Ten give specifics on how the roles
of the mentor, protégé, and boss can be structured to maximize har-
mony in this triangle.

Having Unrealistic Expectations About Promotion

People in one organization that I worked with would not use the
term *candidate* for the protégé because they felt it implied promotion as a result of participation in the program. However, in
some mentoring processes, especially federal government executive development programs, those who complete the activities
successfully and meet clearly stated criteria are promoted. In
other programs, it is understood that even though being a pro-

tégé can enhance one's chances for promotion, it is not a guarantee. In the New York State Department of Taxation and Finance, for example, protégés must still pass the same written and oral civil service tests as their nonprotégé colleagues before even being considered for promotion. To forestall unrealistic expectations on the part of protégés, it is important to clearly communicate to all what participation in the process means—and what it does not mean.

Inability to Take Responsibility

While interviewing people for this book, I heard these comments about protégés' problems from process coordinators (along with the solutions):

- "The mentors sometimes say the protégés aren't assertive enough. So we give them that feedback and tell them to get on the phone and contact their mentors."
- "Some of them lack people skills. We're looking into getting some of them into communication classes so they can make better use of the relationship."
- "When they first take responsibility for developing their own studies, they are full of anxiety. But as time goes on, they become more relaxed. They know how to take on responsibility and find their way around."

These three examples of protégé shortcomings indicate that it is indeed a problem for protégés to become responsible for their own development. But practice, feedback, and formal intervention can make a difference. It takes work to unlearn dependent behavior; accordingly, facilitated mentoring processes do not operate without problems. They can have built-in mechanisms such as careful coordination and evaluation to make adjustments and to enable protégés to take responsibility for their own development.

Jealousy and Gossip from Others

People capable enough to get into prestigious business schools and executive development programs are often labeled by less gifted colleagues as teacher's pets, fast trackers, or jetsetters. However, most ambitious, self-motivated people occasionally hear those comments whether they are in a facilitated mentoring process or not. One protégé whose informal mentor was two levels above her voiced the opinion that a facilitated mentoring process would have actually prevented the jealousy and gossip that she experienced. A structured process would have clearly defined the relationship, making it legitimate and less suspicious in her coworkers' eyes.

Having a Mentor Who Does Not Keep Commitments

"I was lucky. My coach [mentor] was good. But some of the other people in the program had coaches who were worthless. They didn't think it was politically wise to ask for a different coach. So they stuck it out. But they didn't learn anything" (a protégé, confidential interview by the author, 1990). Sometimes mentors do not keep time commitments. Sometimes they do not assist the protégé with developmental activities. Unless there is intervention on the part of a coordinator, the protégé is penalized by the relationship rather than rewarded.

It is crucial to screen, orient, and evaluate mentors. Guidelines for the mentor recruitment and selection process are detailed in Chapter Eight. Those who accept the mentor role must know that the primary reason for the relationship is to develop skills and experience in the protégé systematically. Both protégés and mentors must be evaluated and given feedback during the process in order to make the best of the relationship.

In addition, the relationship must be based on a negotiated agreement that includes, at a minimum

- Explicit description of the skills to be learned and practiced
- The types of activity that will provide this practice
- Agreement on time and frequency of coaching and feedback sessions

If a mentor does not follow the negotiated agreement, clear guidelines must describe how the situation can be handled. The protégé must feel comfortable going to the process coordinator and asking for third-party intervention. This issue is addressed in Chapter Twelve.

Mentor Taking Credit for the Protégé's Work

Every organization has a few unethical people who may take advantage of the unsuspecting. To protect protégés from this possible penalty, it is a good idea to make mentor-protégé projects public. Some processes feature bimonthly meetings chaired by the coordinator, in which both the mentor and the protégé discuss project progress and outline their contributions. In such meetings, skillful coordinator counseling and peer influence can prevent the mentor from taking undue credit for the protégé's work.

Once again, part of the process for the protégé is learning to interact successfully with managers of all kinds, good and bad. If protégés feel exploited, they must be willing and able to approach their coordinators for help. The coordinators can then coach the protégés on strategies for working out satisfactory agreements with the mentors.

People who are interested in having a mentor must take time to consider the potential payoffs and possible penalties. Those who go into mentoring relationships expecting instant magic are soon disappointed. The best of relationships demand communication and problem-solving skills. A protégé who enters a relationship with open eyes and realistic expectations will more than likely get the payoffs he or she is looking for.

Chapter Five

The Mentor's Motivation and Concerns

Keith Elkins likes mentoring so much, he does it full-time. Elkins is a professor at Empire State College in upstate New York, where all faculty are considered mentors (interview by the author, 1990). Typically, Elkins holds individual meetings with each of his full-time students about once a week and each of his half-time students about once every two weeks. Together they draft learning contracts and discuss learning strategies. Each student must come up with an individualized curriculum for obtaining a degree. Elkins's job is to guide and aid the student in any way he can.

"In our initial meeting, I ask the new student three basic questions," says Elkins. "'What do you want to study? Why do you want to study that? How do you learn best?' Sometimes I may sound contentious, but it makes the student think."

Elkins and the student then decide on activities and assignments, which are usually completed on an individual basis. There are no formal lectures or labs at Empire State (H. Hammett, interview by the author, 1990). The student is responsible for designing and completing his or her own educational plan and must help seek out resources to do so. Mentors like Elkins are the student's most vital resource. The Empire State College program is a unique part of the State University of New York system. It is facilitated mentoring at an extreme. Obviously, it works for only the most motivated students—and the most dedicated mentors.

Elkins was initially drawn to the program in 1975 because it fit his own "John Dewey-like" philosophy of education. Now, he sees the costs of such a program. It requires massive amounts of paperwork and coordination on the part of the mentors. Yet Elkins and many of his well-qualified coworkers are not seeking greener academic pastures. What makes them stay? After a bit of thought, Elkins answers. "It sounds a bit self-serving," he says, "but I guess we're just a bunch of cockamamie idealists. This program, even though it's demanding, comes the closest to what we believe education should be. This is a very rewarding place." Indeed, the lesson is that a carefully structured mentoring process—whether in a large corporation or a small volunteer organization—rewards and hence motivates good mentors in many ways.

Benefits for the Mentor

Here are some of the key personal and professional motivators a facilitated process can offer mentors.

Enhanced Self-Esteem

Imagine being asked by a less experienced person to be his or her mentor. The request suggests that you are respected, admired, and noticed in the organization. Mary Helen Rosenstein, who helps manage the mentor program at the New York State Department of Taxation and Finance (interview by the author, 1990), explains that although mentors there participate strictly voluntarily, they must be specifically requested by a protégé before a match is made. "This type of recognition helps the way mentors see themselves," says Rosenstein. "There's a bit of an ego thing going on here, and it's good for the mentor." Observing that others are being requested to function as mentors may be a stimulus to other managers to sharpen their own skills and images.

Revitalized Interest in Work

To the open-minded mentor, a protégé can be a breath of fresh air. A protégé can stimulate the mentor's thinking in new ways about subjects the mentor considered stale. In experience exchanges, mentors spontaneously share what they have learned from their partners—for example, how to communicate with someone in another age group.

"Mentors may actually get more out of the activity than their protégés," says Suzanne Robinson, manager of management development for Planning Research Corporation. "Senior managers [mentors] have clearer ideas about what they are learning from the experience" of meeting several hours a month over a one-year period with their protégés (1990, p. 6).

Close Relationship with the Protégé

I have suggested that many opponents of facilitated mentoring see it as an artificial relationship. However, closeness can develop in a facilitated process. One mentor at Trinity College described her relationship with her protégé this way: "We just talk about things and enjoy them and laugh together. We both thought we had to be real serious, but then [en route to an event together] we began to laugh about all this. When we get together, we tell Trinity stories and just funny things that have happened" (quoted in Kirby, 1989, p. 20).

Closeness doesn't always occur, yet it can be a side benefit. Marilyn Zuckerman, an AT&T quality planning manager, says, "The mentor is there to deal on an emotional level, . . . to impart a greater sense of purpose and to be encouraging" (1990, p. 6).

Financial Reward

Some processes offer financial rewards for mentors. When this benefit is considered, it usually sparks a heated debate. Most mentors quickly say they take on the role because they like helping someone else grow. Yet, in focus groups of potential mentors in which we brainstorm the types of recognition they would welcome, they invariably include money on the list. The best practice seems to be to use some type of bonus points for exempt employees and pay differential for nonmanagers.

Expanded Awareness of the Business Environment

Mentor Plus establishes industry-specific roundtables for small business owners to discuss issues in order to improve business, productivity, management, finances, and so on. The roundtables give business owners a chance to discuss problems and concerns with the consultant and other group members. One member says that "the roundtable allows me to get opinions from people, and, since I have a five-month relationship with them, they know what I'm doing" (Dyrness, 1997).

Fulfillment of One's Own Developmental Needs

Mentors often tell us they learn as much as their partners, particularly in the skills of planning, feedback, coaching, and career management. "They hone their coaching skills," says John Sequeira, manager of Shell Oil Company's mentoring process, "and know the satisfaction of recognizing [that] others can learn from their knowledge, experience and skills on behalf of the organization" ("Mentoring Mentees," 2000, p. 4).

Leaving a Legacy

For executives who want to leave a particular legacy in an organization, facilitated mentoring is a way to do so. We have had recent retirees volunteer to be mentors because they wished to stay in close contact with an organization they had helped to build. In some cases their motivation was enhanced by knowing their retirement income was tied to the continued success of the company. Most of us want a bit more than our fifteen minutes of fame, and passing on our ideas can promote a lasting legacy. Douglas W. Hooper, winner of the 1990 mentor essay contest for high school seniors, described the role mentors have played in his life. He concludes: "Mentors are evident in all our lives. There seems to be with each of us a special person and happening that gives us memories, ideas, and dreams. Through hard work, I hope I will become a mentor to someone" (1990).

Professional Assistance in Business and Work

In many facilitated processes, the protégé completes projects under the mentor's guidance and is thus an added resource for the mentor. One mentor who developed several protégés in his organization admitted that he tries to keep the best ones in his division. Taking an outside viewpoint, Nancy Lewis Heins, president of Change Strategies in Jupiter, Florida, suggests that we need to look at our customers as our mentors because "we will know why we are in business, we will learn how to do our business better, and we can teach our customers how to enhance their business" (1995, p. 2).

T. J. Halatin, assistant professor of management at Southwest Texas State University, neatly summarizes the major benefits to the mentor in this way:

> The supervisor or employee who is a mentor enjoys the intrinsic satisfaction of helping another work toward his or her goals. It is a special moment for the mentor when a subordinate achieves something toward which he or she has worked. The mentor is also able to experience a feeling of self-importance from the respect given by the subordinate, the interest shown in the mentor's stories of past successes, and the treatment of his or her advice by the employee as action guidelines and principles. The respect and appreciation for past efforts by the mentor can lead to a lasting relationship between the two individuals. Through the mentoring relationship itself, mentors can gain information about the organization and operations. Subordinates are natural resources, often willing and eager to share their knowledge. The additional contribution to the organization and its members made as a mentor can also be important to the mentor at evaluation time. Noted will be his or her contribution to the creation of a team spirit within the organization [1989, p. 27].

Concerns for Mentors

Of course, being a mentor can have a downside too. Some processes actually have demotivating factors that test the most altruistic of mentors. Let us now look at some of these issues and propose workable suggestions on how an organization can eliminate obstacles or at least minimize them.

Pressure to Take on the Mentoring Role

A facilitated mentoring process typically recognizes mentors as special, thus making the role an attractive one to people who are capable and want to maintain good standing in the organization. When mentors get added recognition, other managers may feel pressured to volunteer (whether they are suited to the role or not).

A good facilitated process must screen mentor candidates carefully. The manager who prefers spreadsheets to a one-on-one conversation must be counseled by the process coordinator. A good coordinator can help the potential mentor see alternative routes to promotion or recognition in the organization. Unwillingness to screen out inappropriate mentor candidates results in frustration on the part of both the unsuitable mentor and the protégé.

Lack of Requisite Skills

Chapter One described some of the characteristics and skills required of mentors. For example, the mentor must be able to coach, tutor, give feedback, do career planning, and assist the protégé in specific activities. It is possible that a mentor candidate lacks a critical skill—say, the ability to plan a career path—but is excellent in other ways. Because this person is understandably reluctant to reveal lack of knowledge or skills, tactful measurement of specific skills is a necessary, although complex, task. Strategies can then be used to build the missing skills in a suitable candidate. In our example, the potential mentor can be scheduled to participate in an orientation process that includes information on career planning. In addition, the coordinator must be willing to act as a resource and be able to coach when the mentor is not performing satisfactorily.

Not Taking the Coaching and Feedback Role Seriously

Coaching is at the core of the mentoring process. What exactly is coaching? The mentor must be able to direct the protégé to relevant activities and projects. The mentor must be able to say what is going well and where more practice is needed. The mentor must be able to differentiate competent from not-yet-competent behaviors of the protégé. This discrimination suggests that the observed performance is assessed against some standard, which is a functional definition of appraisal—letting people know how they are doing relative to an agreed standard. For feedback to be most effective, it must be based on objective appraisal, include positive reinforcement of desired behaviors, and include modeling of or instruction on those behaviors to be improved. Mastery of appraisal, coaching, and feedback skills is essential and fundamental to this task. If there is any question about the strengths of a potential mentor in these key areas, some form of training in coaching and feedback must be included in the orientation.

The protégé can also influence the quality of the coaching and feedback by asking the mentor for assistance in specific tasks. For example, if the protégé is to make a major presentation to a prospective client, the protégé may ask the mentor to listen to a practice session and give some pointers on how to handle potentially troublesome parts of the talk. Further, the protégé may ask the mentor to sit in on the presentation and give feedback at a later time. This committed interaction, initiated by the protégé, is highly likely to be taken seriously by both the protégé and the mentor.

An excellent example of real-time coaching was related to us by a pair that had gone on sales calls together. When the protégé missed a point in describing benefits to Kelly, the customer, the mentor said to the protégé, "And perhaps Kelly would like to hear about how this will add value to the distribution system." This immediate coaching enabled the protégé to be more successful and gave the mentor an opportunity for positive reinforcement when they debriefed the contact.

In addition, organizational procedures can influence the mentor role. If the mentor's ability to coach is appraised regularly, the mentor takes the coaching responsibility seriously.

Lacking Time to Work with Protégés

Many experienced managers and administrators cite developing others as their primary responsibility. When one top-level executive was asked how he fit meetings with a protégé into his work schedule, he answered, "I'm always in a mentor role, both formally and informally. My role is to help my subordinates make decisions. I let them bounce ideas off me and I give my input. But ultimately, I want them to be able to make their own decisions. If I were making all their decisions for them, I wouldn't need them, would I? So taking on what you call an 'additional protégé' is no great hardship for me in terms of time. It's what I do anyway" (S. Hefter, interview by the author, 1990).

Not all managers have this philosophy. Some managers who assume the mentor role become so busy with their own work that they give the protégé interaction low priority. When there is a time crunch, the first meeting canceled is the one with the protégé.

This attitude can be countered if the mentor's time with the protégé is linked to performance appraisal and if the coordinator tracks meeting times and frequencies. The process must help the mentor make time with the protégé a high priority. Some organizations with goals for time to be billed to clients or to projects establish a billing code for the mentor and protégé to use for their time together. This procedure sends a clear message that the organization values developing people. With regular feedback, mentors can learn to use their time creatively to meet regular work demands and the needs of the protégé. Depending on the nature of the formal agreement, face-to-face meetings with the protégé may be monthly, with telephone contact in between. The mentor who feels put upon to keep appointments may not be the best mentor, or it may not be a good time for taking on the mentor role.

Also, mentors can turn the protégé into their own time-saving resource by delegating meaningful work to the protégé. The automotive service technicians (Garcia and McCrary, 1997) quickly learned that the student interns could do a lot of the tasks in service work and enable the technician to take on more jobs each day. The compensation was based on jobs completed rather than straight hours, so the service technician mentor then earned more. This strategy serves a dual purpose. It frees up time for the mentor while developing the protégé's work skills.

No Perceived Reward, Benefit, or Payoff

Lack of rewards for the mentor is one of the most commonly mentioned obstacles to structuring the mentoring process. Dynamic, impatient leaders let you know quickly that there must be something visible in it for them if they are to make a significant time and energy investment in a function that primarily benefits others. A mentor with little motivation may simply drop out of the job.

As noted, some mentors are amply rewarded by the knowledge that they are contributing to the growth and development of another person. Other mentors need concrete rewards to sustain their involvement. In either case, people tend to repeat those activities that result in some reward; therefore, even though it takes some effort and creativity, rewards for the mentors can and must be designed into the process.

The importance of making mentoring part of performance appraisal has already been discussed at length. Professional recognition of a good job should be included in the mentor's regular progress reviews. At 3M, the mentor role itself is a reward, a role that is earned and respected (Halatin, 1989). In other organizations, promotions or financial advancement are a direct outcome of the effort spent in mentoring. For example, in California teachers in some school districts can earn up to $70,000 by agreeing to be mentors. In industry, bonus points may be awarded for sustained satisfactory performance as a mentor.

Another way to reward mentors is through public recognition. If your organization has a newsletter or periodical, you might include a Mentor of the Month story. Examples of particularly noteworthy assistance can be gathered from the protégés. Publicity about the process can also include biographical sketches of or statements from people who serve as mentors. This public recognition of competence and leadership can be a powerful reward.

Possessiveness of Protégés

Occasionally a mentor identifies so strongly with a protégé that he or she becomes jealous and possessive. The mentor then undermines the interaction between the natural boss and the protégé. The mentor who competes for the attention and time of the protégé, emphasizing the priority of their relationship over the protégé's regular work duties, creates a divisive situation. When the protégé gets caught up in making comparisons between the mentor and the boss, and the boss loses, the whole situation deteriorates.

Several techniques can be used to keep the mentor's perspective in line. First, a negotiated agreement between the protégé, mentor, and natural boss must clearly outline the work expected of the protégé. If the protégé is to perform all regular duties during the mentoring relationship, emphasizing this expectation in the agreement helps to invest the mentor in the protégé's regular work assignment. Second, the duration of the relationship must be stated in the agreement. The mentor is then aware of the finite nature of the formal relationship. Finally, it is of the utmost importance to keep communication channels open between the protégé, the protégé's natural boss, the mentor, and the coordinator. If possessiveness surfaces, the mentor must be reminded of the purpose of the relationship.

Not Letting Protégés Take the Risks Necessary for Learning

When the mentor has a strong vested interest in the protégé's success, the mentor may also be tempted to take on some of the protégé's tasks. If a project is highly visible, the mentor may want the protégé to look good for the mentor's sake and overstep the fine line between guidance and doing work for the protégé. There is some element of risk in most learning situations, but experience is in fact the best teacher. In orientation and feedback sessions, mentors must be reminded that guided learning can increase the likelihood of success for the protégé and enhance the protégé's self-esteem. It is the mentor's role to guide and advise—not to do.

Protégé Resentment

A person who openly expresses the desire to learn, grow, and advance in the organization may be a threat to a manager who is at the next higher level. For this reason, managers sometimes ignore the potential of a direct report—or worse yet, throw obstacles in that person's path.

If the mentoring process is designed to support succession planning and advancement, a relatively easy way to avoid this pitfall is to match the protégé with a mentor who is at least two levels higher.

In flatter organizations, this solution may not be possible. But additional distance can be engineered by matching mentors with protégés in other departments or functions. Yvonne Shepard, a mentor at AT&T Bell Laboratories (1989), finds that having a protégé from another department helps her bring objectivity to the relationship that a supervisor might not have.

If you are thinking about becoming a mentor or if you are structuring a facilitated process, review this summary of benefits for the mentor:

- Refined interpersonal skills. Mentors hone their own skills for effective interaction with others.
- Self-esteem enhanced; psychic rewards; pride in helping others grow.
- The experience of helping another to grow instills pride in the helper.
- Enhanced status in the organization. Mentors are respected for the valuable role they play in developing future leaders of the organization.

- Increased awareness of the caliber of employees, their core competencies, and the talent pool available for staffing decisions.
- Job enrichment with unusual projects. In a stable or downsizing organization, a mentor who has mastered the job finds enrichment in projects that are outside usual responsibilities.
- Additional work accomplished.
- Career advancement. The mentor may get promoted because of effective people development.
- Financial rewards. Bonuses or other financial incentives may be given to those who take on the extra task of functioning as a mentor.
- Creative input for ongoing work.
- Avoiding burnout due to routine work or overwork.
- Maintenance of motivation when on a plateau. The fresh viewpoint of the protégé may renew the enthusiasm and motivation of the mentor.
- Public recognition and acclaim. Publicity about the existence and effectiveness of the mentoring process brings added recognition of the stature of the mentor.
- Expanded awareness of the organization structure and operations.
- Extended influence over the mission and direction of the organization.
- Mentors in tune with what is really happening at the worker level, with no filter in between.

If you are still interested in a facilitated process after reviewing the benefits and the possible downside for mentors, go on to Part Two for the how-tos.

Part Two

Facilitated Mentoring
How to Make It Work

Part Two describes mentoring processes in several types of organizations. Illustrations of the key components of each process are included in Chapter Six. The activities that take place in each component are described only briefly here and discussed in detail in Chapters Eight through Thirteen.

Models and Applications

Figure 6.1 in Chapter Six presents an illustration of the implementation flow of a generic process. This example includes most of the essential activities one would encounter in a facilitated mentoring process, although an organization is likely to have more or fewer key components in its process. Figures 6.3 through 6.8 in that chapter illustrate six other models, each of which applies to a specific organization. Some of these programs have been in operation now for a number of years. Some have disappeared owing to changing priorities in the organization. I've kept them in this edition of the text because they illustrate a useful variety of mentoring processes in public and private sector organizations, educational institutions, and nonprofits. Objectives for each are stated.

Model Number One (Figure 6.1)

Generic implementation flow of components in a facilitated mentoring process. Adapted from work processes developed by MMHA The Managers' Mentors.

Model Number Two (Figure 6.3)

Executive Candidate Development Program (ECDP) in the U.S. General Accounting Office (GAO). The GAO has approximately 5,100 people on staff, with 125 at the senior executive level. Fifty to sixty candidates apply for the ECDP each year.

Model Number Three (Figure 6.4)

Public sector mentoring program (the organization's identity is kept confidential). Small, specialized group in a federal agency with a need to prepare successors for a function that requires a high degree of skills and independent responsibility.

Model Number Four (Figure 6.5)

RINA Accountancy Corporation (formerly Rooney, Ida, Nolt and Ahern, Certified Public Accountants, a member of Midsnell International) is a full-service public accounting firm headquartered in Oakland, California. There were approximately one hundred people on the professional staff when the mentoring process was introduced.

Model Number Five (Figure 6.6)

Trinity College Mentoring Program in Washington, D.C. The primary goal of the program is to offer selected student mentees (protégés) the opportunity to work with a mentor in a professional area related to her academic major or career interests.

Model Number Six (Figure 6.7)

Tumor Registrars Association of California (TRAC). Application of a facilitated mentor process in the field of health care, pairing hospital-based professionals with association volunteers. In 1985, California passed a mandatory reporting law requiring all new cancer cases to be reported by certified tumor registrars. The objective of the mentoring process is to increase the level of productivity in the tumor registries and the quality of care provided to patients.

Model Number Seven (Figure 6.8)

Empire State College in New York. Since 1971, the faculty has been designated as "mentors" to define a new role in higher education. The mentor program objective is to have mentors and students develop learning contracts for guided, individualized studies that lead to undergraduate degrees.

How to Make It Work

After you have reviewed each model, you will be familiar with most of the procedures associated with facilitated mentoring processes. Our research and experience prove that with careful design, administration, and evaluation, a facilitated mentoring process can maximize benefits and minimize risks in the right organization. What is the right organization? Chapter Seven helps you answer that question.

Chapters Eight through Thirteen describe the basics of the facilitated mentoring process. These chapters cover all the components of the generic implementation flow presented in Figure 6.1. Each chapter ends with a checklist of the key factors influencing implementation of the component discussed in the chapter. Use the checklists to jot down ideas that help you prepare for successful implementation.

Issues

In many of the workshops we do on facilitated mentoring, we ask people to finish the sentence "It won't work here because . . . ." This exercise generates many concerns, most of which have been dealt with in this book already. But other, sensitive issues continue to be voiced. Don't mentors and protégés often fall in love? If the process is only for women and people of color, aren't we risking alienating our other employees? Does their jealousy fuel racism? How do unions react to such processes? Chapter Fourteen attempts to answer such questions and to describe practical ways to approach issues such as the relationship between the mentor and protégé, and management and organizational issues. Chapter Fifteen gives a concise checklist of key considerations in planning for a successful mentoring process. A gap analysis, which we call readiness assessment, is the starting point for that plan.

Chapter Six

Mentoring Models and Applications

In Part One, you read about the many benefits and the most likely problems for organizations, for mentors, and for protégés when the mentoring process is facilitated. To realize fully the beneficial results of facilitating the mentoring process, it is important to implement a process designed to function successfully and to avoid problems. Preventive actions and remedies for pitfalls can help guarantee a smooth, successful process most of the time. Figure 6.1 illustrates a generic implementation flow that contains the major components of a good mentoring process.

Looking at this linear flow may mislead one to believe that this is how the process works. The way the process actually operates is illustrated in Figure 6.2. This graphic makes it easier to see the roles and relationships of the participants. It also indicates that the mentoring process is just one strategy for improving results, and that it must be aligned with other strategies such as recruitment, hiring, placing, paying, formal training and development, and recognition.

Other applications and variations of mentoring programs are illustrated in Figures 6.3 through 6.8, later in this chapter. If you are considering a facilitated mentoring process or just want to learn how a good one works, scanning these illustrations is the place to start. This chapter tells only what is taking place in each program. The following chapters give details on how to implement a facilitated process and manage each component in your organization.

Figure 6.1. Facilitated Mentoring Implementation Flow.

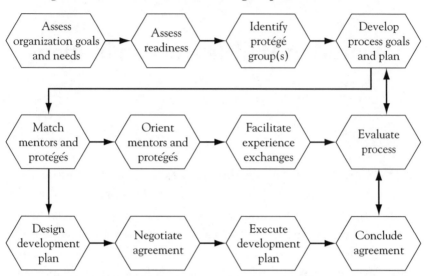

Source: Adapted from MMHA The Managers' Mentors, Inc. Copyright © 1972, 2000. Used with permission.

Generic Implementation Flow for a Facilitated Mentoring Process

Figure 6.1 illustrates a comprehensive facilitated mentoring process that can be implemented in many types and sizes of organization. Each of the components is described briefly here.

Assess Organization Goals and Needs	Consideration of any intervention must start with the goals, needs, and opportunities that the organization is facing. Determining the desired state and the actual present produces the data to describe the gap and realistically decide which intervention, if any, is most appropriate. This assessment can be done with an environmental scan, along with gathering data from key decision makers and opinion setters.

Figure 6.2. Illustration of the Operating Concept of Facilitated Mentoring.

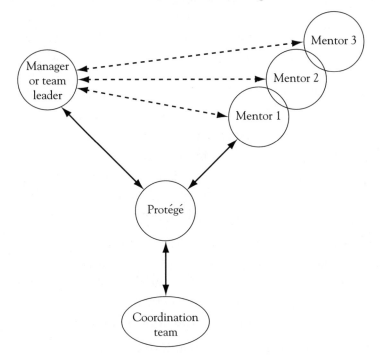

Source: MMHA Facilitated Mentoring Model and Processes. Copyright © 2000. Used with permission.

Assess Readiness	This step gathers data on the environment within which the mentoring process is to thrive. The degree of commitment and support for the process is analyzed and the alignment with other performance improvement processes determined. Individual and focus group interviews with executives or administrators capture data needed here.
Identify Protégés	In this step, the organization identifies the priority groups of people who are eligible for the current mentoring process—for example, by targeting women in supervisory production

jobs who can be groomed to move into management positions. One program identified its target group as engineers who lacked state-of-the-art technical skills. Other examples are candidates for senior executive positions, or any new employee who wants to take advantage of such developmental assistance. Individual protégés may volunteer, be nominated by a boss or other sponsor, or compete for selection through application and testing. The protégé's identity and agreement to participate can be entered into a record or database for tracking the results of the mentoring effort.

Develop Process Goals and Plan

In this step, the outcomes sought from the mentoring process are documented. An action plan and timeline are created to guide the coordination team and other participants throughout the implementation.

Match Mentors and Protégés

A mentor is tentatively matched with a specific protégé after consideration of the experience, skills, and knowledge wanted by the protégé and the ability of the mentor to provide practice or guidance in those areas. Compatibility of styles and personality can also be a factor in the selection.

Orient Mentors and Protégés

The most eager and competent mentor must still be oriented to the role. A well-designed orientation can get the protégé off to a good start as well. Time commitments, types of activity, time and budget support, relationship with the natural boss, and reporting requirements are some subjects typically included in the mentor orientation. The design may also include skill practice for mentors on feedback and coaching, and for protégés on assertiveness training and career planning.

Design Development Plan

Ideally, the protégé has drafted some career goals and development objectives before asking for a mentor. Input from the manager or team leader is useful. The draft plan is improved in discussion with the mentor as the pair negotiates its working agreement.

Negotiate Agreement

A clear agreement is an essential foundation of a good mentor-protégé relationship. It can be a written agreement, or it can be a discussion bound only by a handshake. Whatever the form, it should include a confidentiality requirement, the duration of the relationship, the frequency of meetings, time to be invested in mentoring activities by each party, and the specific role of the mentor.

Execute Development Plan

The protégé and mentor then work through the development plan as negotiated in their agreement. This step is the core of the mentoring process and continues as long as the protégé wants to have assistance. Some mentoring pairs communicate by telephone or electronic messages more than in face-to-face meetings.

Facilitate Experience Exchanges

The coordination team often convenes experience exchange meetings for mentors and protégés to discuss performance planning, coaching, and feedback sessions. The frequency of the meetings depends on the nature of the relationship. It may also be influenced by the geographical proximity of the pair. These sessions can yield important data for process improvement and learning progress.

Conclude Agreement	A mentoring relationship established to promote developing specific skills or competencies has a sunset clause built in. The relationship may also be concluded if either member of the pair believes it is no longer productive for the two to work together. It is important to provide a mechanism for dissolution without attributing fault to either person. This is referred to as the *no-fault conclusion*.
Evaluate Process	This step takes you back to the gaps that the mentoring process was designed to fill, and the goals set for it. Both formative and summative evaluation data are useful for process improvement and reporting results.

This example is but one of many effective designs for facilitating the mentoring relationship. You may have scanned it thinking that it is a perfect fit for your organization, and you can use it as a framework for designing your process.

If, however, you want to design your process with additional or other activities, see the possibilities in the following sections. Our research has brought a number of successful mentoring processes with varied structures to our attention. Figures 6.3 through 6.8 illustrate six of them, in government, accounting, education, and health care. They use a variety of formats for effective facilitation of the mentoring process. You may find that one of these processes matches what your organization requires.

ECDP for the U.S. General Accounting Office

Figure 6.3 illustrates the mentoring program at the senior-executive level in a large federal agency, the U.S. General Accounting Office (GAO). The primary objectives of the program are as follows:

Figure 6.3. Executive Candidate Development Program (ECDP) for the U.S. General Accounting Office.

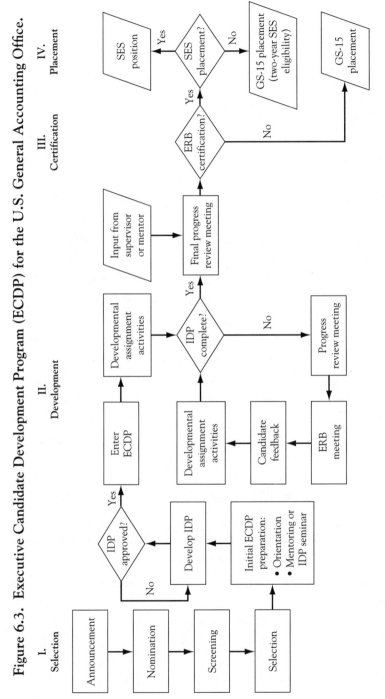

Source: Program coordinator, Executive Candidate Development Program, U.S. General Accounting Office. Used with permission.

- To provide the agency with a pool of candidates capable of being executives
- To give the candidates the knowledge and understanding of the organization necessary for successful performance
- To ensure that the executive candidates demonstrate excellence in managerial and technical areas

The Executive Candidate Development Program (ECDP) has four phases: selection, development, certification, and placement. Here are brief descriptions of the activities that take place in each phase.

Phase One: Selection	Openings in the ECDP, based on the assessed needs of the agency, are announced at specified times during the year. Division or office heads then nominate as candidates (protégés) those senior managers who appear best qualified for executive positions. A pool of mentors has in the meantime been created from volunteers who were screened and qualified by the Executive Resources Board (ERB). Sometimes a mentor outside the GAO is selected because of specialized skills and experiences. Applicants are screened by the Qualifications and Performance Review Board. Qualified applicants are ranked by quartile and recommended to the ERB. The ERB makes final recommendations for selection into the program.
Phase Two: Development	Selected candidates participate in an orientation seminar, and an Individual Development Plan (IDP) or mentoring seminar. The IDP is drafted by the candidate, with guidance and counseling by the mentor and the training institute staff, for approval by

	the ERB. Developmental assignments and activities are carried out by the candidate with feedback from the mentor and supervisors, and through regular progress-review meetings with the ERB.
Phase Three: Certification	The ERB monitors the candidates' progress in the program and makes judgments on certification of the candidates for executive positions.
Phase Four: Placement	The Senior Executive Service (SES) placement decision is made by the ERB with input from supervisors and division or office heads.

Small Public Sector Mentoring Program

The program in Figure 6.4 was designed for a small, select group of particularly skilled people in a department of the federal government. In this agency, one job is staffed by specially trained people who develop a high level of expertise during their two-to-three-year rotational assignments. Because of the organization's request for confidentiality, the department cannot be named, nor can specific examples that would indicate the nature of the organization be disclosed. But this program is relevant for any organization that needs to groom people for a position requiring special skills. Examples include high-level positions in the financial professions, high-risk jobs such as chemical plant operator, and service positions such as insurance claims adjuster.

Mentors Identified	In this type of organization, the skilled and experienced job incumbent is the only available mentor, and the only one who can pass on to a new employee the expertise required to perform adequately in the job. Thus, all job incumbents are considered mentors. The option of volunteering is not available.

Figure 6.4. Public Sector Mentoring Program.

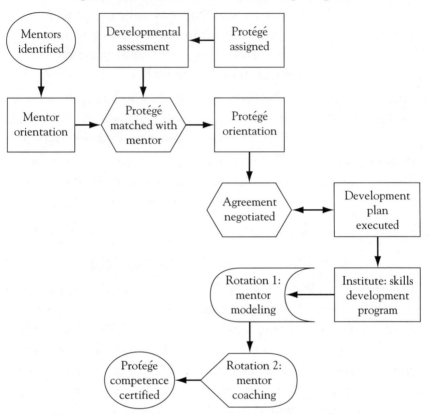

Mentor Orientation	The orientation is especially important when using this model, as the mentors may not have well-developed interpersonal skills. Their expertise in the technical aspects of the job may be unquestionable, yet they may not have had any opportunity to coach and give feedback. The orientation is designed to include training and practice in these essential skills.
Developmental Needs Assessment	The technical skills needed by protégés in this model are evident and are already specified. Because the organization is

training people to do a certain job, it is easy to overlook other developmental needs without systematic assessment of the candidate's strengths and deficiencies. Such an assessment is necessary to design and plan a customized development process.

Protégés Matched with Mentors

This step takes place only if there is more than one position to be filled. Because the skills to be learned are already known, the emphasis here is on making the best match of work styles and personalities. It may not be possible to switch mentors if this relationship does not work.

Protégé Orientation

This activity includes all the typical orientation features described in the generic model. Particular stress must be given to timely execution of the development plan because it is likely that the mentor will be leaving the position at a scheduled time and not be available for further coaching.

Agreement Negotiated

The agreement in this model is particularly important, again because the mentor is likely to be moving on. The meetings and coaching sessions must be firmly fixed.

Development Plan Executed

In this model, there is high risk for the protégé. Often the assignment of the protégé overlaps that of the mentor for only a short period of time, so the protégé might not have sufficient time to learn the necessary skills. Consequently, any planned developmental activities outside specific job duties may be given secondary priority by both the mentor and the protégé.

Protégé Institute	The design includes a dedicated time of formal training for the protégé at a training institute. The content of such training may be both job-specific and generic. As part of it, the mentor may be involved with coaching the protégé on individual study activities.
Mentor Modeling	An initial period of time is set aside for the mentor to model or demonstrate all the skills and competencies to be learned by the protégé. The protégé is an observer and learner during this phase.
Mentor Coaching	During this part of the process, the protégé takes the active role with the mentor acting as coach. In a high-risk situation, the potential hazard is mitigated by having the experienced person available as the protégé builds confidence.
Protégé Competence Certified	The mentoring relationship concludes when the competence of the protégé is certified, or when a decision is reached not to certify the protégé for the position. It may also conclude when the transfer or departure date for the mentor is reached. In such cases, protégés can be matched with other mentors to continue the training.

Mentoring Program for a Small Accounting Firm

Figure 6.5 illustrates a program designed for a small accounting firm, RINA Accountancy Corporation (formerly Rooney, Ida, Nolt and Ahern, Certified Public Accountants), headquartered in Oakland, California. This program was born when the firm recognized the staff's need for guidance and support in achieving personal and professional goals. Program goals include the following:

Figure 6.5. Mentoring Program Activity Flow
for RINA Accountancy Corporation.

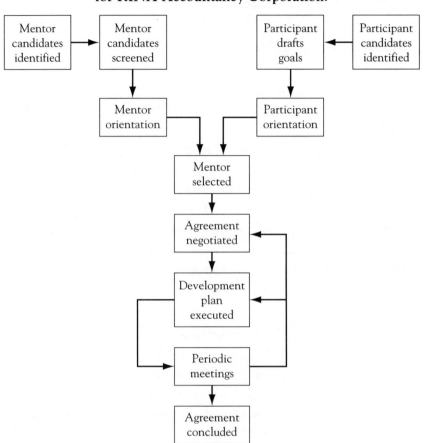

Source: Graphic designed from Rooney, Ida, Nolt and Ahern, Certified Public Accountants, mentoring program description. Used with permission.

- Communicating firm policies and expectations to staff
- Assisting staff in identifying opportunities for growth and specialization offered within the firm
- Assisting staff in setting, monitoring, and achieving congruent personal and firm goals
- Assisting staff in career-development decisions
- Responsively addressing problems encountered by staff

- Increasing job satisfaction
- Assisting in developing staff
- Encouraging sharing of experiences and use of talents among all members of the firm

The program is available to every one of the one hundred employees voluntarily and is administered by the personnel manager. Because staff members have short-term serial assignments with managers who are in charge of an audit or tax review, the firm wanted a process that would add a consistent focus on individual development activities. The mentoring program was implemented to meet this need. Identification of mentors and *participants*, as protégés are called in this program, proceeds simultaneously. Most of the components of the generic implementation flow are applied in this program. The descriptions here cite specific differences from that example.

Mentor Candidates Identified

The goal is to have an adequate pool of mentors to make timely and appropriate matches with participants. Mentors volunteer to participate, sometimes at the suggestion of the managing partner or other senior staff. Volunteering indicates interest in the program and willingness to function as a mentor.

A call for volunteers is extended twice each year, and anyone may volunteer at other times. For example, if the firm hires a manager with particular expertise in management information systems, this person could quickly be matched with another member of the firm for mentoring and coaching on information systems.

Mentor Candidates Screened

The personnel manager receives the names of five mentor candidates from each person who wants to become a participant (protégé). Essentially, the participants are screening the mentors, as the program's goal is to match participants with their first or second choice. The presumption is that the nominated mentors have the skills and abilities wanted by the participants.

Mentor Orientation

This program had one large orientation for mentors and participants in the beginning. The mission, goals, and projected growth of the firm were described, as well as how the mentoring program supports the mission and goals. Policies and procedures relevant to promotion were part of the orientation, as was the availability of educational and developmental resources. The orientation included details of the mentoring program (such as development plans, types of agreement that might be negotiated), recognition for mentors, and a description of the coordinator's role.

Individual orientation to the program takes place when a new employee joins the firm. At that time, all these subjects are discussed, and the individual has the opportunity to express interest in the program.

Participant Candidates Identified

As stated, the program is open to any employee. Typical characteristics and responsibilities of the participants, such as willingness to assume responsibility for one's own growth and development, are published in the personnel manual.

Participant Drafts Goals

Participants are expected to draft a statement of developmental needs, set goals, and formulate an action plan for discussion with the mentor.

Participant Orientation	As stated, the initial orientation was a group session for both mentors and participants. As new people join the firm, they learn about the mentoring program in the basic orientation for new staff members.
Mentors Selected	The goal is to match every participant with his or her first or second choice of mentor. A matrix of the mentor-participant relationships is maintained by the coordinator, who works with department heads and other leaders of the firm to determine the most appropriate matches.
Agreement Negotiated	An outline of the subjects to be included in the agreement is given to all interested participants and mentors. Some pairs elect not to use the suggested format as a record of the agreement, although most use it as a guide for the discussion.
Development Plan Executed	During the course of the relationship, the participant is expected to maintain documentation on developmental goals, action plans, and accomplishments. Regular contact with the coordinator is a part of the plan and the responsibility of each participant.
Periodic Meetings	The mentor-participant pairs are expected to meet regularly for planning activities, coaching, and feedback. The firm picks up the tab for lunch for some of these meetings. In addition, the coordinator chairs periodic meetings with mentors and participants.
Agreement Concludes	The relationship can be concluded at the agreed time or when either party can no longer meet the specified obligations. It may also end ahead of the established time if the

participant attains all goals set with the current mentor and wants to develop different skills or knowledge with another mentor.

College Mentoring Program to Introduce Students to Work World

Figure 6.6 represents the Trinity College Mentoring Program in Washington, D.C. The primary goal of the program is to offer selected student mentees (protégés) the opportunity to work with a mentor in a professional area related to her academic major or career interests. Additional outcomes are the following:

- Students have a professional role model.
- Students have a view of work in a profession.
- Students have access to someone who has been through college, job, and family transitions.
- Mentors give something back to Trinity.
- Alumnae keep up with Trinity and its students.
- Alumnae give ongoing attention to their own careers.
- Mentor program presents the college as one that works.

The program differs from an internship in that work skills or experience need not be the primary focus. Mentors are expected to provide support, encouragement, and important perspectives on issues that women face in today's professional world. It is also hoped that lasting career networks and friendships result.

Two important components help manage and structure this program. The director coordinates the day-to-day aspects, such as contacting mentors and students, and managing the database and mentor-mentee orientations. The Mentor Program Committee, which is made up of faculty and the current executive director of the Alumni Association, acts in an advisory capacity to the director. For example, the committee members usually know the mentee

Figure 6.6. Trinity College Mentoring Program.

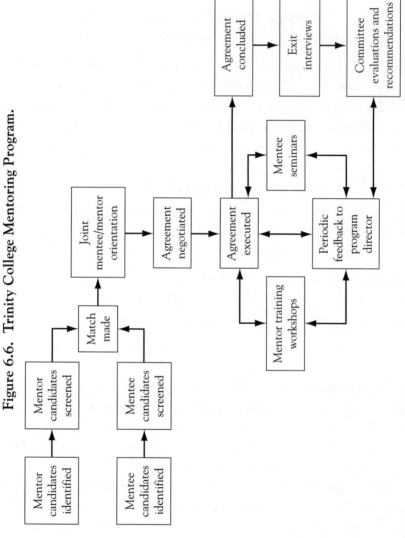

Source: Graphic designed from Trinity College program description. Used with permission.

candidates and mentors quite well. This personal knowledge helps in the mentor-mentee screening and matching process. The committee also advises on problem resolution and program changes.

The committee chair, Mary Hayes (interview by the author, 1990), reports that the program is a great success and will be a permanent service of the college. Both potential mentors and student protégés are overwhelmingly interested in keeping the program going. Here is how it works.

Mentor Candidates Identified

A letter and questionnaire are regularly sent out jointly by the Trinity Career and Counseling Center and the Alumni Association. The purpose is to identify alumnae who wish to become associated with Trinity's Career Network. The database is national, and alumnae are asked to identify the areas in which they wish to be of service: lectures, internships, career panel presentations, the mentor program. Potential mentors are initially identified from this list and are asked to volunteer by returning personal and professional background information.

Mentor Candidates Screened

Mentor candidates are screened by geographical area. Only alumnae who live and work in the metropolitan Washington, D.C., area are put into the mentor pool. A database includes information such as class, employer, undergraduate, graduate, and professional degrees.

Mentee Candidates Identified

Mentees self-nominate yearly. Any sophomore student who is not studying abroad in her junior year may apply. Two letters of recommendation must be sent in addition to a written application.

Mentee Candidates Screened	Applications and letters of recommendation are reviewed. In subsequent interviews, potential mentees are advised of program requirements. Generally, all self-nominated students are allowed into the program unless their interest, motivation, or academic status is questionable. For example, of seventeen applicants in 1989, only two were not accepted and that was because they missed interviews.
Match Made	The Mentor Program Committee usually matches mentor and mentee on the basis of the self-diagnosed professional needs of the mentee. If for instance the mentee states an interest in a marketing career, she is likely matched with a former business major or a marketing professional.
Joint Mentee- Mentor Orientation	The mentor and mentee meet at a group reception or orientation. During this gathering, presentations are made about program expectations.
Agreement Negotiated	The mentor and mentee decide on the types of activity they work on together. The director makes general suggestions, but the actual agreement is set by only the two parties.
Mentor Training Workshops	During the course of the relationship, mentors attend one formal workshop and at least one informal social event, which cover role orientation, expectations, and training. Mentors share their experiences and discuss relationship issues.
Mentee Seminars	Mentees attend three seminars each semester that focus on career-related issues. They also do personal assessments and participate in assertiveness training.

Periodic Feedback to Program Director	The director keeps in constant contact with the mentor and student to monitor the relationship. If problems surface, the director may ask the Mentor Program Committee for procedural advice.
Agreement Concluded	The relationship continues for three semesters and ends with the conclusion of the mentee's first senior semester.
Exit Interviews	Mentees are interviewed by two committee members to gather data about the program and the mentor's performance.
Committee Evaluations and Recommendations	The Mentor Program Committee evaluates the interviews and recommends any policy or procedural changes to the director.

Mentoring Program in Health Care

Figure 6.7 is a model for a mentor program in the field of health care. It pairs new or inexperienced tumor registrars with experienced ones. The mentor program is run by the Tumor Registrars Association of California (TRAC), a joint professional and volunteer organization. Tumor registrars have the primary responsibilities of identifying, registering, and reporting cancer cases. They record demographic data and also information on type of cancer, stage of the disease, and treatment. The registrars follow up these cases yearly to record the progress of treatment. Tumor registrars must have a basic knowledge of anatomy and physiology along with skills in data collection and analysis of cancer data, and knowledge of cancer management.

A 1985 California state law requires that health care professionals and organizations report all cancer cases to the Department of Health Services. This information is used by the state to track incidents of cancer, causes, and survival rates. Since the

Figure 6.7. Tumor Registrars Association of California Mentoring Program.

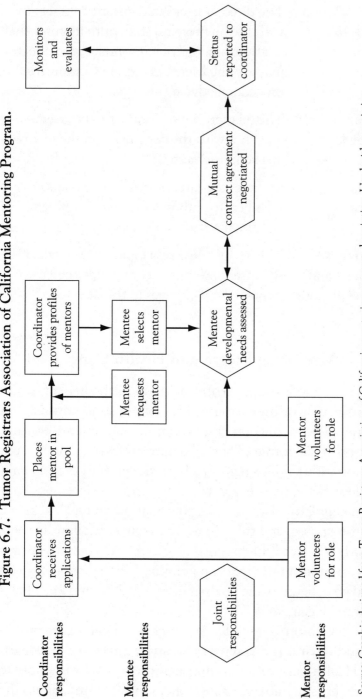

Source: Graphic designed from Tumor Registrars Association of California mentoring program description. Used with permission.

mandatory law was passed, the need for experienced tumor registrars has increased. The TRAC program was developed to increase the skills and confidence of new tumor registrars by allowing them to network and consult with experienced role models who offer guidance and serve as resources. The basic program goal is to augment the formal education of protégés, which is a two-year college curriculum, or their formal training in basic registry skills. Two other objectives are to help protégés meet state certification requirements and increase the level of productivity in tumor registries.

The policies and procedures have been carefully and professionally designed to work in an unusual environment that includes both paid professionals and unpaid volunteers. Criteria have been established for mentors and for mentees (protégés). An evaluation process is built into the program, and ongoing data are collected. Figure 6.7 outlines the major responsibilities of the coordinator, the mentee, and the mentor. Here is a brief description of these activities.

Mentor Volunteers for Role	Mentors must have five years' experience in the field and be certified tumor registrars. They complete applications and supply letters of reference.
Coordinator Receives Applications	The coordinator, who is appointed by the education committee chair, screens applications from mentor candidates and places those who are chosen in a pool.
Mentor Participates in Orientation	All approved mentor volunteers attend an orientation program that includes information on goals, criteria, operating structure, and skills assessment.
Mentee Requests Mentor	A prospective mentee submits an application to the coordinator, stating prior experience, training, and areas of need.

Coordinator Provides Profiles of Mentors	Based on mentee developmental needs and geographical proximity, a list of qualified mentors is sent to the mentee upon application to the program.
Mentee Selects Mentor	From the profiles of qualified mentors, the mentee, once chosen, makes a selection and works out an agreement with the mentor for the developmental activities desired.
Mentee Developmental Needs Assessed	Jointly, the mentor and mentee assess the developmental needs of the mentee.
Mutual Contract Agreement	After verbal acceptance, a written contract specifying the services to be provided is signed by both parties.
Status Reported to Coordinator	Quarterly reports are made to the coordinator by both the mentor and the mentee. A final report is sent at termination of the agreement.
Monitoring and Evaluation	The coordinator monitors all operations of the program through review of applications, telephone contact with mentors and mentees, review of contracts, and status reports. Mentors are evaluated yearly, and the entire program is evaluated by the education committee.

Mentoring Program at Empire State College

Since its founding in 1971, Empire State College of the State University of New York (SUNY-ESC) has employed mentoring for academic advisement and instruction. The college maintains a core faculty at seven major centers throughout New York State. Faculty mentors at SUNY-ESC, representing many disciplines in the arts and sciences, assist students (who are professionals and working adults) in developing personalized degree programs. The term *mentor* was adopted by the faculty not only as a conscious variation within the teaching profession but because its rich variations also mirror the roles that mentors play outside of higher education in companies and organizations (H. Hammett, interview by the author, 1989). Mentors and students (protégés) employ learning contracts to create guided, individualized studies. This flexible mentoring program, illustrated in Figure 6.8, has these objectives:

- Adult students design rigorous and relevant learning programs with mentors.
- Students have control over the pacing of college studies, enabling them to balance job, home, and school obligations.
- Learning at work is linked with formal college studies.

Here are the components of the mentoring process at Empire State College.

Student Contacts SUNY-ESC	A potential student contacts the college.
Student Information Session	Potential students attend an information session and receive an application and financial-aid materials.
Student Applies	Application is received and accepted by the college, and student is invited to an orientation.
Match to Mentor	An associate dean reviews the student's application and the mentor data and makes a match with a primary mentor.
Student Orientation	The student then attends orientation, meets the primary mentor, and enrolls in the program.

Figure 6.8. Empire State College Mentoring Program.

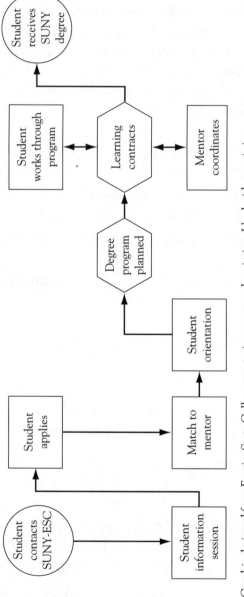

Source: Graphic designed from Empire State College mentoring program description. Used with permission.

Degree Program Planned	Student and mentor assess prior learning and plan a degree program.
Learning Contracts	Student and mentor then negotiate a series of learning contracts. All contracts are reviewed by the dean or associate dean (N. Hanawi, interview with author, 1989).
Student Works Through Program	The student works through the learning activities with the primary mentor and other faculty mentors.
Mentor Coordinates	Throughout the progression of learning contracts, the mentor serves as guide, coach, and adviser and suggests other learning experiences.
Evaluation	Both the primary mentor and the student write a narrative evaluation of what the student has learned in the process.

Key Process Components

In the beginning of this chapter, Figure 6.1 illustrated the implementation flow for a facilitated mentoring process; the illustration contains most of the components that research and experience suggest a successful process should have. Our recent experience shows that it is important to add the readiness assessment component at the beginning; this is described in Chapter Seven. The evaluation component must also be highlighted in communicating how the process works best (see Chapter Thirteen). In those and other following chapters you will find detailed guidelines for designing and implementing the processes described.

Chapter Seven

Assessing Needs and Determining Organizational Readiness

This chapter assumes that you believe facilitated mentoring is a good, workable way to develop people. Now you have to decide whether it will work in your organization. To make that decision, you must first establish what goals, needs, or opportunities your organization is facing that convince you there is a gap that a mentoring process will fill; and second, determine whether the culture of your organization will support such a process. As the experiences related in previous chapters show, a successful facilitated mentoring process requires careful planning, commitment, and support. The steps outlined in this chapter help you determine your organization's readiness for such a process.

Determine Your Organization's Future Succession Planning Needs

Are there any data to justify a mentoring process in your organization? Does your organization really have a significant gap between desired and actual outcomes that a mentoring process will fill? One way to answer these questions is take a good look at your future personnel needs through succession planning. Succession planning is more than projecting your future human resource requirements. It also means designing strategies for preparing people who are now in the organization to fill those requirements, and perhaps recruiting experienced people from external sources.

When you do succession planning, keep in mind that all the data you are analyzing are about the past. What you have always been doing may not be a relevant approach in today's volatile environment. Try to avoid being constrained by past history, no matter how good the results were or how comfortable the old, familiar ways of doing things are. Because succession planning is about the future, you require more than historical data to make the most useful projections for your organization.

Good succession planning also involves looking both at your organization and at the larger environment in which it operates. What factors nearby and around the globe have an impact on your organization's goals? Trends, especially the current labor shortage and the increasingly multicultural nature of the workforce, must be considered. Recent U.S. Department of Labor reports (1999) confirm what Elizabeth Dole, secretary of labor, warned in her "State of the Workforce" address in 1990: "The skills of a large number of experienced workers are now obsolete or soon will be made obsolete by changes in technology. . . . There is no doubt that our work force crisis is a challenge to education, labor, business, and government" (1990). Are you expecting significant technological changes in your industry or in the equipment you use? Technological changes can create a demand for new skills, unusual knowledge, and different attitudes.

Is your company a target for a takeover or merger? What will changes in world trade agreements do to the demand for your product or service? Perhaps your company is mounting an aggressive acquisition campaign to grow the business. Obviously you will not be analyzing each of these indicators in depth in preparation for designing a mentoring process. We mention these external factors at this point to prompt you to consider the broad spectrum of challenges in creating an organization that can get results today and tomorrow. In the end, succession planning means creating plans to perpetuate your organization.

This is not meant to be an exhaustive list of the issues and concerns of your organization today, but it can trigger you to think of specific impacts you may anticipate. Not even the most skillful and knowledgeable planners can anticipate all the possible variables. The best that can be done is to gather the most accurate data available, write down the assumptions that are made about both the data and the future, and then make plans using the combined judgment of a planning team.

You can use several methods to assess the number and type of employees your organization needs. Prange and Smalley (1988) outline several techniques for making workforce projections that are practical even for small organizations. They caution that each technique is a different way of thinking about the future, and each yields its own projection. They describe four techniques:

- Trend extrapolation
- Delphi probes
- Scenarios
- Precursor forecasting

Trend extrapolation plots past data with discovered curves extrapolated into the future. This technique is applicable for estimating attrition from aging and retiring employees.

Delphi probes are polls of experts done several times to obtain a consensus of intuitive estimates of the future. Such combined guesses can prove valuable, or they can be an accumulation of ignorance. Those selected for their intuition about future employment factors might be economists, demographic researchers, international business and commerce experts, and futurists.

Scenarios involve writing a story about or description of the future, usually telling how to get there from here. Visioning or speculating in this way may be appropriate when you anticipate that your organization will be strongly affected by technological or social change.

Precursor forecasting assumes a correlation between events in various environments. For example, an economic downturn has a negative impact on sales of big-ticket or gift items such as luxury automobiles. The manufacturers of these products and suppliers of raw materials for them can then expect a slowing demand in their own industry. By looking at these precursors, the manufacturers of necessity goods, such as clothing, food, and building materials, can also predict the timing of slowdowns in their industries.

You can use one technique or a combination of them to get the greatest utility out of your estimate of people needs for the next five or ten years. Keep in mind when projecting human resource requirements that you are looking for more than numbers. You also want to know what kind of skills your employees must have to do the job.

The next question to answer in succession planning is, Where will we get these employees? Do your projections for movement of current employees indicate that an adequate number are ready to be promoted to supervisory and management positions? Are current recruitment and hiring practices producing the required number of people with the types of skill desired? Finally, do current practices allow the organization to meet its goals for a workforce that mirrors customers and community and brings diversity of education, creativity, and thought processes? If the answers to these three questions are no or maybe, you have some justification for a structured mentoring process. If your preliminary decision about mentoring is a go, continue your readiness assessment by taking a close look inside the organization at the beliefs and values of the managers.

Examine Commitment to
Human Resource Development

The acid test of a commitment to developing people is whether upper-level managers would rather grow competence than buy it. Today in countries such as Ireland, Taiwan, and the United States, buying technical talent is very costly; sizable hiring bonuses are the norm. Visible evidence of top-management support is critical to the success and continuity of a mentoring process. When executive management believes that a development program makes a difference, the program will be given high priority by all members of the organization. You probably already have some feeling for your organization's commitment to human resource development. The last time you were scheduled to attend a training workshop or seminar out of town and a crisis occurred at work, did your boss say, "Sorry, but we need you here"? Or was the message "That training is important; we can handle things here"?

A mentoring process does not typically have such visible costs as the registration fees for an outside workshop. However, allowing the mentor and protégé to meet and engage in important coaching and feedback discussions may initially have an impact on productive time. If a commitment to allowing time to be used for development activities is not already firmly entrenched in the organization, facilitated mentoring is probably not a good idea.

Determine the Scope of the Mentoring Process

The next factor to assess is the scope of the proposed mentoring process. Does the need for developing people extend across all functions and down through all levels? Is this a long-term need? Or is there a temporary need to facilitate developing a special target group for new product development or building a management team for an acquired company?

The advice of most experienced users of mentoring processes is to start small and expand after a period of successful operation. This tactic gives you a process of manageable size while you accumulate experience and work out the kinks in your policies and operating procedures. Our current best practices suggest that a beta test of twenty to thirty pairs yields sufficient evaluation data to determine value added, as well as reveal needed improvements in the processes or resources. This trial period can be used to get feedback, work out problems, and keep motivated mentors and protégés from repeated discouraging experiences.

Assess the Organization's Ability to Sustain the Characteristics of Successful Mentoring Processes

Continuing study of mentoring processes has revealed some characteristics that are essential for their success. A quick way to assess your organization's readiness for a facilitated mentoring process is to determine the degree to which a number of characteristics can be successfully sustained in your environment. Let's look at these characteristics one by one.

Voluntary Participation

Almost everyone with firsthand experience in a mentoring process, and many who have researched them and written about them, stresses voluntary participation by both mentor and protégé. The necessary enthusiasm and commitment does not occur when mentors and protégés are drafted. On an individual level, the recommendation is that people be invited to become involved and not be forced to do so if they are reluctant to participate.

➜ *Look for volunteers, not draftees.*

Skipped-Level Mentors

If one goal of the process is to support succession planning, does your organization have sufficient numbers of people to match protégés with mentors who are at the appropriate level? Some distance minimizes the possible concern of a mentor that a protégé is out to get his or her job. A protégé who is at the next level below can be too close for comfort—a competitor—to the mentor.

➜ *Identify a pool of mentors at appropriate levels for the targeted protégé group.*

Cross-Functional Pairing

It is sometimes complicated to administer pairing across functional lines in an organization, but the benefits are many. A mentor from another department brings broad experiences that enhance learning for a protégé. Also, when the protégé has targeted a future position in another department or function, it is advantageous to select a mentor from that area. Knowledge of the skills required for jobs in the target area are relevant for the protégé. In addition, the communication and political network in the new department can be readily accessed with the help of a mentor who has been working there. The ideal mentor also has experience in the protégé's current department or function.

→ *Look for mentor candidates across functions.*

Flexible Duration

Many factors influence the duration of each relationship:

- The protégé's development objectives
- Frequency of contact
- Type of skill to be learned and practiced
- Geographical proximity

Whatever the agreed time period, it must be long enough to meet the needs of the protégé and short enough to coincide with the availability of the mentor. The protégé who simply wants exposure to a department needs less time than one who wants to work on a long-term project with a mentor's help. Thus, the time period should be adjustable within set parameters determined by the protégé's goals. My suggestion is to let learning be the constant and time be the variable.

→ *Set a flexible conclusion date that meets the protégé's needs.*

One-on-One Mentoring

This recommendation, like all the others, must be kept flexible. Many competent and experienced mentors function in two or more relationships all the time. In the beginning it is wise to keep the mentoring on a one-to-one basis until the novice mentor has a chance to gauge how much time will be spent in the role. There is lots of discussion today about "group mentoring," with one mentor meeting with a group of people to share experiences. Group processes are more efficient when many people have the same skill gaps. A group process can make a person with unique skills and competencies available to numerous people in a short period of time. The most significant drawback to a group process is that if the participants are not open and candid about experience or skill deficiencies, they will not grow and gain as much as can be achieved in a one-on-one interaction.

→ *Keep the mentor with one protégé until experience, competence, and willingness allow the mentor to take on more.*

No-Fault Conclusion

If the mentoring relationship doesn't jell or if it turns sour for either party, there must be a way to conclude it without damage to anyone. This feature must be part of the policy and procedure and should be emphasized during the orientation and agreement negotiations.

→ *Establish and emphasize the no-fault conclusion at the beginning of the process.*

Integration with the Total Development Effort

If the mentoring process is a separate, special process, the responsibilities for it and for other human resource development activities tend to become cloudy. When mentoring is seen as one module of a comprehensive development process, though, it can be readily integrated with the career-planning, training, and other development activities already offered in the organization: "Separate programs are extremely vulnerable to economic downturns, budget cuts, and changes of affection. Only an integrated, facilitated process linked to current and future missions or business imperatives can be expected to stand the buffeting of the winds of change" (Murray, 1998).

→ *Look for ways to integrate mentoring into existing human resource development programs.*

High Priority for Evaluation

Top management must support continued evaluation of the process. The evaluation format and strategies should be designed at the beginning in order to collect uncontaminated data for comparison. To start the process, a database of current results in recruiting, hiring, training, and promoting people throughout the organization must be established. Chapter Thirteen outlines possible types of data you might want. Tracking the results of mentoring processes can be done through periodic reports from mentors, protégés, and natural bosses, through interviews, through analysis of promotions, and in other ways.

Evaluation does two things. Most obviously, it provides important information on how well the process is working, and the value added. It also yields data on how to continuously improve the quality of the process. It can be an important tool in getting organizational members to buy in. For example, operational managers tend to abdicate responsibility for developing their people because they have been led to believe training is the role of the training department or a similar function in human resources. In order to emphasize the manager's responsibility for training and developing subordinates, the mentoring coordinator must insist that the manager or team leader be an active participant in development planning and in negotiating the agreement with the mentor, and also in assessing how well that plan worked.

→ *Give mentoring process evaluation a high priority.*

Creation and Communication of Policies and Procedures

A task force or process advisory board may be established to work out policies and procedures. This approach is particularly valuable when the process is to be available to anyone in the organization and when it is likely there are cross-functional pairs. An advisory board of high-level managers or administrators who represent each of the functional areas can collaborate on a design to maximize the benefits and minimize the risks. In a presentation at the 2000 annual meeting of the International Society for Performance Improvement, Kay Stiles of Chevron Information Technology described strategies for establishing a Guidance Review Team (GRT) and getting its ongoing support: "The key points are to research best practices, both internally and externally, and to develop a compelling business case for mentoring" (Stiles, 2000).

➜ *Create and communicate clear policy and procedures.*

Communication Plan

It is important that the organization clearly communicate what the process is and is not. This is the component most often overlooked in the mentoring implementation plan. The communication can be both informative and motivational. The information must include the criteria for participation, the policy for engaging in development activities on company time, what (if any) guarantees are included for successful protégés, how the mentors are rewarded, and how to get out of a bad situation. In addition, promotional communications can create enthusiasm for involvement. Building a positive image of the mentoring process stimulates support and participation by mentors, protégés, bosses, and others.

➜ *Create a plan to communicate the process and promote participation.*

Checklist

If you glance back at this list of important considerations, you can see that establishing a structured mentoring process is a serious commitment. Exhibit 7.1 asks important questions that help you determine your organization's readiness for facilitated mentoring. On the checklist, write the actions you can take to get the information you need to make this important decision. Obviously you will identify other factors that influence the readiness of your organization. Add those items to the checklist so you have a complete action plan when you finish.

Exhibit 7.1. Checklist for Determining Organizational Readiness.

Action to Take

1. What personnel needs do we have that would justify starting a facilitated mentoring process? _____

2. Are top-level executives prepared to commit time and money to human resource development? In what visible ways will they make this commitment? _____

3. What is the scope of the proposed pilot process in terms of
   - Target group?
   - Functional areas?
   - Levels?
   - Duration?
   - Size?
   - Duration of each relationship? _____

4. Will voluntary participation work here? _____

5. Are there enough mentors, and at appropriate levels? _____

6. Is cross-functional pairing desirable? How do we administer it? _____

7. Can the duration of each relationship be flexible? _____

(Continued)

Exhibit 7.1. Checklist for Determining Organizational Readiness, Continued.

Action to Take

8. Is a no-fault conclusion acceptable? _____

9. How does facilitated mentoring fit
   with other human resource develop- _____
   ment programs? _____
   _____

10. Is one-on-one mentoring possible? _____

11. Is evaluation given high priority? _____

12. Who establishes policies and _____
    procedures? _____

13. What are the available communi- _____
    cation media? _____

Other questions

14. _____   _____
     _____   _____

15. _____   _____
     _____   _____

Chapter Eight

Structuring the Mentor Role

Qualifications, Recruitment, Selection, and Rewards

The mentor role deserves your most careful attention, as the mentor's wholehearted participation is critical to the effectiveness of the mentoring relationship. Competence and commitment are the unequivocal characteristics of a successful mentor. Qualifying candidates for the mentor role must build from a foundation of being willing and able to help another person to grow. The types of capability and the nature of the commitment vary with each mentor-protégé relationship.

Many educational organizations are selecting mentors for both students and teachers. Their processes have the potential for tremendous impact on the participants, and for societal good. Eleven sponsors (including the National Education Association, American Federation of Teachers, National PTA, National School Boards Association, and others) are contributing greatly to the 21st Century Teachers program, which is designed to train one in every six teachers in the nation on using technology in the classroom. One hundred thousand teachers with computer experience were recruited by officials to ensure the success of the program through mentoring (Page, 1996).

Having read this far in the book, you probably have some good ideas about using mentors in your development programs. You have also, no doubt, already thought of the many obstacles you may face in implementing your mentoring process. In this chapter, you will find specific guidelines for defining the role of the mentor, for recruiting mentors, for creating the mechanisms for establishing a pool of qualified mentors, and for making the men-toring role work well.

For every guideline suggested here, you could probably find an exception in a mentoring process somewhere. For example, I have talked with people who have had successful peer mentoring rela-tionships and with others whose mentors were younger than they were. In one orientation workshop, I observed a young male "techie" entering into a mentoring partnership with a senior female executive. He had technical skills she needed for results analysis, and she had organizational experience and business acumen that would prove valuable to him.

Likewise, there are many examples of bosses who function as mentors to some of their subordinates. In *Managers as Mentors*, Chip Bell focuses on managers taking on the role of mentor to their own subordinates: "Perhaps the most contributive role of today's leader is that of mentor" (Bell, 1996b, p. 19). Bell offers a mnemonic to symbolize the transfer of wisdom by the mentor— SAGE, which stands for

Surrendering control

Accepting as an act of inclusion

Gifting in generously bestowing something on another

Extending (meaning, pushing the relationship beyond expected boundaries)

An important caution about the mentor's dual role is voiced by Anne Brockbank and Nic Beech, who studied thirty-five managers and their mentors in a hierarchical contractual relationship over an eighteen-month period of time in the King's Healthcare NHS Trust in London. "The problems experienced in these cases," they report, "suggest that line managers do not make the best mentors, and that such relationships could be better served by someone who wouldn't normally directly influence the mentee" (Brockbank and Beech, 1999).

Perhaps the only unbreakable rule about facilitated mentoring is that the process be designed for maximum flexibility and to fulfill the needs of the organization. For clarity and ease of description, the processes described in this chapter follow the generic facilitated mentoring model presented in Chapter Six.

Qualifications

An individual may be a superb role model and do all of the things a sponsor does, yet not have the skills to perform effectively as a mentor. Several specific skills and attributes necessary to carry out the functions of a mentor have emerged from our experience with designing, implementing, and evaluating mentoring processes for management-level people. The following are the hallmarks of a master mentor (Everitt and Murray-Hicks, 1981):

- Strong interpersonal skills
- Organizational knowledge
- Exemplary supervisory skills
- Technical competence
- Personal power and charisma
- Status and prestige
- Willingness to be responsible for someone else's growth
- Ability to share credit
- Patience and risk taking

When the mentoring match has been made for the purpose of transferring technical or professional skills, some of those characteristics are less important. Many organizations are experiencing rapid changes in technology used for everything from analysis of results to distribution of products. The requisite competencies must sometimes be hired into the company, and these expert hires must take on the role of mentor to transfer the skills to others in the organization. Technically oriented people may not have what one would immediately describe as personal power and charisma; however, if they are skillful in communicating with one person, they can successfully transfer the desired knowledge and skills.

Use the brief descriptions of the characteristics in the next subsections to help you recognize the most likely mentor candidates in your organization. Keep in mind that the reason for the match makes the characteristic more or less relevant. Each description is followed by the key element to look for.

Strong Interpersonal Skills

Mentors enjoy being with people; they like interacting with others. The potential mentor is the animated talker in the middle of a group, not the solitary figure off on the sidelines engrossed in a newspaper. Because the mentor role demands close relationships, the best candidate is one who enjoys working with people more than working alone or working with things.

Of course, there are always exceptions. An individual may be unusually skillful in a professional or technical area—for example, research methodology—and not have good communication skills. A persistent protégé may be able to extract the desired assistance from such a person. But beware of pairing a passive protégé with a strong, silent type as mentor. One of the two must be capable and willing to initiate contact and work at keeping the relationship going.

→ *Look for a person who talks and listens.*

Knowledge of the Organization

The most helpful mentor is one who has intimate knowledge of the vision and long-range goals of the organization. To access this information, the mentor must have an open line to the formal and informal communication channels within the organization.

Having a mentor who is able to tap into an extensive network of movers and shakers can significantly expand the resources available to the protégé. Knowing where the organization is going (and how quickly or slowly) enables the mentor to assess the reality of the protégé's aspirations. The mentor knows where the opportunities are in terms of projected growth, direction, and goals of the organization. If the organization is downsizing, the mentor can direct the protégé into appropriate areas, such as a lateral move into another function.

→ *Look for a person with an extensive network of resources.*

Skills

Certain management skills seem to be essential for competent performance as a mentor in most relationships. Again, when the goal is technical skill transfer, the mentor may not need all of these skills:

- Planning performance—helping others set objectives, create action plans, estimate resource requirements, and schedule time
- Appraising performance—observing another's performance, evaluating it, and determining the appropriate type of feedback
- Giving feedback and coaching—providing feedback that clearly reinforces desired performance or coaches to improve performance to agreed standards
- Modeling—demonstrating desirable techniques for task performance
- Delegating—determining appropriate tasks to be delegated to a person capable of performing those tasks; negotiating agreement on the tasks to be performed, time for completion, authorities to be consulted, and resources to be used

At this point you might be thinking, *Why are these skills especially important in a mentor?* Everyone who supervises the work of others should have these skills! Of course they should. However, many people are promoted to supervisory positions because they are the best workers. In all fields—craft, technical, and professional—many people without supervisory experience or skills are assigned to jobs that require overseeing the work of subordinates. Rarely is a person's leadership potential assessed in any systematic way before a promotional decision is made. Furthermore, few people are prepared or trained for the supervisory role. The misconception is that if they can do the work, they can also get it done through others. This situation is not likely to change in the near future, so it is important to carefully screen mentor candidates for basic competencies in the areas of planning, feedback, listening, and coaching. It is not enough to want to be a mentor. One has to have these skills, or be willing to develop them in preparation for the mentor role.

➔ *Look for a person who has managed groups of people successfully, or who has chaired committees and task forces.*

Technical Competence

It may seem obvious that the mentor should be competent in the skill area the protégé wants to develop. However, certain organizations have set up mentoring programs and made matches on the basis of the mentor's position and the protégé's membership in a target group. Little or no thought is given to the skill deficiencies of the protégé and none to the relevant competence of the mentor.

Ideally, the mentor is skilled and experienced in two or more functions of the organization. The mentor who draws from a broad background can offer the protégé a variety of examples and deep, rich experience. In addition, the mentor with extensive experience is less likely to see the protégé as an immediate rival for promotions or other perks.

➔ *Look for a person who has skills the protégé needs plus skills in at least one other technical or professional area.*

Status and Prestige

The status of the mentor may be unimportant when the relationship is invisible to others. But when a process is public and designed to groom people for increased responsibility, the mentors must have prestige and know how to share it with their protégés.

Why should mentors be prestigious? First, it is more likely that a higher-status mentor knows the organization well enough to guide someone else. Second, a basic principle of behavior modeling is that people are likely to emulate someone who is perceived as having prestige. Few people consciously imitate the actions of a person regarded as a bad example. The development process is easier and more efficient when the mentor is held in high esteem than when he or she is not.

➜ *Find the person who makes the news and is respected.*

Personal Power

Positive regards and respect for others in the organization make the mentor a powerful magnet of leadership. This quality is sometimes called charisma. It is easy to recognize those who have it and those who do not. People are quickly attracted to the charismatic leader. It may be part of that mysterious attraction that is often cited as the genesis of informal mentoring relationships. Although the manifestations of personal power may be learned behaviors, these are not skills that can be readily taught.

➜ *Look for the person whose opinions are sought.*

Willingness to Be Responsible for Someone Else's Growth

You cannot draft people to be mentors. The tangible and intangible rewards of helping someone else grow make some people willing and eager to accept such an awesome responsibility. Some managers share my opinion that people are ultimately responsible for their own growth and development; however, the policies and practices of many organizations have taught people that they cannot be responsible for themselves. Self-management is discouraged when employees are told what to do and when to do it, what to learn and when to learn it. Although we read and hear a lot about empowerment of individual employees, the majority of organizations are still traditionally managed and do little to encourage self-responsibility for growth and development.

As an interim step, the organization, the individual's boss, the mentor, and the individual can share responsibility for development. One of the preeminent researchers on feedback and coaching, Don Tosti, has good advice for mentors who wish to help someone grow: "If you believe you have the right to give someone feedback, you must also assume the obligation to make sure that feedback is usable and useful. Avoid feedback that only compares people with each other. People need to know their best targets of opportunity for improvement" (e-mail to author, Sept. 8, 2000).

A mentor who is secure about his or her own competence is likely to be generous with time spent in helping others to grow. It may be an added incentive to remind mentor candidates that it adds to their credentials to be seen as a star maker.

→ *Look for a person who initiates coaching contacts with others.*

Ability to Share Credit

The exceptional mentor demonstrates that there is sufficient credit and recognition for everyone to share. This superstar can step out of the limelight and let the protégé take the bows. Good mentors neither claim the protégé's work as their own nor attribute their own work to the protégé.

→ *Look for a person who talks and behaves teamwork.*

Patience in Risky Situations

Patience when the risk of failure is high may be the most important—and the least measurable—attribute of all. Having the patience and courage to let a protégé risk and fail, all the while being there to provide support, takes unusual fortitude. Perhaps the most important function mentors have is creating the opportunities for protégés to prove themselves in risky situations (Collins and Scott, 1978). But they must also be prudent about those risks and let protégés develop at their own speed. There is a fine line between knowing when to allow a protégé to muddle through and knowing when to offer help. A mentor who jumps in too quickly may be pushing or stifling the protégé's development.

→ *Look for a person who says, "Give it a try!"*

It may seem impossible to find all these qualifications in the mentors you are seeking. The best suggestion is to get as much as you can, and expect to help the mentors develop additional skills as they prepare to work with the protégés.

Recruitment Strategies

In any discussion of facilitated processes, the first thing people ask about is the source of mentors. Where will they come from? Who is willing to give the necessary time and energy to work diligently to help someone else grow? Important reputations and large egos are on the line. What if things don't work out? What if those who do accept give only lip service to the role without spending quality time with the protégés? Sometimes these questions are not asked aloud, but the issues lurk as potential obstacles to the success of the process.

The people who complain about the dearth of mentors may be looking in the wrong places and at the wrong people. Look around you, not just at the highest levels. To find people throughout the organization who are willing to help others by mentoring, consider these recruiting strategies: use volunteers, or use nominations by executives or by the protégés themselves.

Using Volunteers

Using volunteering as a strategy for recruitment entails having clearly stated criteria. Fortunately, most people know whether they enjoy instructing and coaching. But not everyone possesses the ability to make an objective assessment of his or her own readiness to carry out all the necessary mentoring responsibilities. Use the qualifications described previously in this chapter to develop a list of criteria for your mentor candidates. Add to the list any specific technical or professional skills you require. Exhibit 8.1 is a sample call for volunteers.

Exhibit 8.1. Sample Call for Volunteer Mentors.

Everyone is encouraged to develop the skills and competencies to function effectively as a mentor. Mentors are asked to volunteer for the *mentor pool.* Mentors are expected to have most of these characteristics:

- Willingness to assume and visibly demonstrate leadership

- People-oriented behavior

- Regarded as being successful in the firm

- Willingness to assume responsibility and accountability as a mentor

- Knowledgeable about the firm's goals, policies, functions, communication channels, training programs, and so on

- Willingness to help set development goals, coach, and give feedback

- Awareness of resources available within and outside the firm

- Committed to developing staff

- Willingness to share personal experiences relevant to the needs of the participant

Source: Adapted from Everitt and Murray-Hicks (1981).

Using Nomination by Executives

Another option for recruiting mentors is to have top management and administrative people nominate candidates for the mentor pool. Nominators should use published criteria when considering and selecting these nominees. At RINA Accountancy, a small accounting firm where every high-level person is well-known to the others, the managing partner, senior partners, and department heads are asked to provide an initial list of nominees for the mentor pool. The coordinator, who is head of the personnel department, screens the list of nominees along with the names suggested by participants (the title used for protégés) to make the initial matches and to build a pool of available mentors for later additions to the professional staff.

Using Nomination by Protégés

In the GAO (R. Glazer, interview by the author, 1989), the mentoring process is administered by a panel that asks the candidates (protégés) to nominate three people whom they would like to consider as their senior adviser (mentor). When one of the three is matched with a candidate, the other two may be asked to be members of the mentor pool and be considered by other candidates. In this way, the pool of potential mentors is expanded as the number of active relationships grows.

Making It Workable and Rewarding for Mentors

Maintaining the motivation of mentors is a critical factor in sustaining the process. Other keys to success are described in the following discussion.

Select the Title for the Role of Mentor

Your choice for what to call the mentor's role depends on how you structure the mentor role and on the organization's culture; in turn, the term you use influences how the role is carried out. For instance, *exemplar* suggests that the mentor may be expected only to model behaviors for the protégé. The term *coach* implies that the mentor is involved in specific skills-training activities. Most organizations in the countries in which we work are comfortable with (and are using) the term *mentor*. Even with this now familiar term, though, there are still many myths and misconceptions about what the role really entails.

Describe the Responsibilities

Make the description of the mentor role factual and realistic. It is tempting to make the mentoring role sound glamorous, which can raise some unrealistic expectations about the benefits. Include in this description the number of protégés the mentor is expected to work with at any time. As noted in Chapter Seven, I recommend one mentor to one protégé unless the mentor is extraordinarily skilled and has a lot of surplus time. Specify the type and frequency of reporting that is required, if any. Include an estimate of the time the mentor may be expected to spend in developmental activities with the protégé.

Advertise

Develop promotional pieces suitable to the communication vehicles available to you to publicize the existence, features, and benefits of your mentoring process. Soliciting volunteers necessitates spreading the word as widely as possible. Consider word of mouth, e-mail blasts, periodic newsletters, union newspapers, management reports, training catalogs, posters, and desk-drop leaflets. Publish endorsement of the process by high-level administrators or managers.

Make It Easy to Respond

Prepare a simple form for volunteers or nominators to use. The amount and type of information you require varies depending on the structure of your process and the size of your organization. You want enough information to make it relatively easy to match the mentor's experience and capabilities with the protégé's developmental needs. Ask for at least this much information:

- Name
- Current location
- Education
- Experience
- Why interested in the mentor role
- Type of mentoring relationship wanted
- What specific skills or experiences willing to transfer
- Amount of time available for mentoring activities
- Any constraints on location or timing

Screen Candidates for Readiness

Amend the hallmarks of master mentors at the beginning of this chapter (under the heading "Qualifications"), and use the list as an initial screening checklist to assess the readiness of the volunteers and nominees for the mentor pool.

Make the Match with the Protégé

A review of the preliminary development plans of the protégés reveals the precise experience and skills sought in the mentors. Mentor candidates who have passed the initial screening can be contacted for additional information—skills, experience, abilities, and availability—that is relevant to the needs of a specific person who is seeking a mentor.

Making It Work

Mentors' motivation is also affected by their understanding of their role and responsibilities. How you recognize and reward mentors directly influences their performance in the role.

Orient Mentors to the Role

A group orientation session may be most efficient when the process is first established. Later it may be practical to have the coordinator brief the new mentors individually. A sample outline for a mentor orientation session is included in Chapter Eleven.

Make It Matter to the Mentors

The rewards you offer have a major impact on the mentors' motivation. Some of the ways you can build rewards into your process were described in Chapter Five. The surest way to induce the mentor to take the role seriously is to tie the mentor's performance to the regular appraisal process. This performance objective can then be negotiated with the mentor's boss and tracked for progress and feedback.

The protégé can be a valuable source of feedback on the quality and timeliness of the mentor's performance. Financial rewards may be in the form of bonuses, stock options, or paid time off. Nonfinancial, yet visible and powerful, rewards include a trip, featured recognition in a publication, a certificate of merit or contribution, attendance at a special educational program, and tickets for an entertainment event. More than one thousand AYES master technician mentors were given engraved wrenches and a letter of congratulations in recognition of their contributions to the success of their student interns, their dealerships, and the AYES initiative (D. I. Gray, e-mail to author, Sept. 7, 2000). Never underestimate the power of a gold star.

Maintain Records on the Mentor Pool

If your organization has an accessible personnel database, use it to keep track of volunteers or nominees. Explore with your information technology people how to put the mentor profiles into an online database that can be searched by key words. This database can be used later to track the relationship after matches have been made.

Checklist

Careful recruitment and selection of mentors can increase the potential for your process to succeed. Use Exhibit 8.2 to jot down specific actions you can take to ensure a good structure. Be realistic and specific in the actions you plan to take.

Exhibit 8.2. Checklist for Structuring the Mentor Role and Creating the Mentor Pool.

Action to Take

1. What term will we use for the mentor role? _____

2. How do we recruit mentors? _____

3. What are the basic characteristics we want mentors to have? _____

4. How do we recognize and reward mentors? _____

5. How do we use promotional material to attract mentors? _____

6. How can we make it easy for people to volunteer or respond to the nomination process? _____

7. Which process do we use to screen the mentor candidates' skills:
   • General?
   • Relationship-specific? _____

8. What systems do we have, or need, to record and maintain the mentor pool? _____

9. What do we include in the description of the mentor's role? _____

10. How can we ensure that mentors share credit with protégés? _____

11. How can we ensure that mentors let protégés take the risks necessary for learning? _____

12. How do we orient mentors to the role? _____

Other questions

13. _____   _____

14. _____   _____

Chapter Nine

Selecting Protégés and Diagnosing
Their Development Needs

One of the most frequently cited and important benefits of facilitating mentoring is the increased likelihood of success for the protégé. Achievement is one of the key motivators. When you can ensure success through the guidance of a mentor, the enthusiasm and motivation of the protégé are sustained. In addition, because protégés have fewer failure exercises than do people who are not protégés, the organization's cost for grooming talented people to take on new or increased responsibility is reduced. This chapter helps you identify the protégé group, screen and select the protégés, and diagnose and make plans to meet their specific needs.

Identifying Protégé Candidates

Chapter Seven discussed the use of succession-planning techniques to identify major protégé target groups. For example, an organization in which many executives will retire in the near future might target second-line managers who have the potential to move up. If necessitated by the organization's goals to mirror its customer base or community, this target group might be further narrowed to women and minorities in lower-level positions.

Once you have determined the target group, your next task is to identify individuals who will take personal responsibility for their own growth and development. The most popular strategies used to locate candidates are self-nomination, boss nomination, sponsor nomination, and automatic placement of new hires.

Self-Nomination

Perhaps the easiest way to identify protégés is to issue a call for self-nominations. Those who nominate themselves are likely to be motivated and capable of self-directed growth.

When using this strategy, it is important to communicate clearly the criteria for participation, responsibilities, and expected outcomes of the process. For example, the TRAC program (see Chapter Six) clearly states in its application form that to volunteer one must, among other things, be a TRAC member in good standing, abide by a statement of mentee responsibilities, and not take any financial reimbursement for participation in the program.

Failure to make criteria and conditions clear is likely to create a horrendous workload for the process coordinator. Trinity College (see Chapter Six) found that excluding any student who planned to study abroad in her junior year reduced the number of applicants by 50 percent. This new criterion made administering the process easier because it ensured that the mentoring relationship would not be interrupted by students' travel, and it reduced the number of applications to be processed and relationships to be monitored.

Stating protégé criteria serves another important purpose. It can save you the task of telling those self-nominated candidates who are not yet ready that they are not viable candidates for the process. Explicitly stating all criteria for the process before announcing that people may volunteer often prevents having unqualified people apply.

Boss Nomination

The second strategy for identifying protégés also requires that objectives and criteria for participation be clearly and widely publicized. With the strategy of boss nomination, managers and supervisors are invited to nominate candidates to participate in the process. The succession-planning group could also issue a request that people be identified who have the potential for promotion in specific areas. The request may be made openly through a memo, a management bulletin, or a newsletter. If the process is not open to everyone, direction for nomination of protégés may come from operating officers to managers at the next tier in a closed meeting, a confidential memorandum, or a personal conversation.

Keep in mind that bosses often have blind spots as to the potential of their subordinates. If you have any concern that some managers or supervisors may be less than enthusiastic about nominating their own people, the process coordinator can make direct contacts with bosses to encourage developing their people.

Sponsor Nomination

The third strategy, sponsor nomination, avoids the blind spot or bias of a boss. It allows any astute observer to nominate a candidate. Input can come from leaders in every function of the organization. However, if you are looking for a particular set of protégé experiences, skills, and interests, the coordinator might best go only to managers or administrators of the most relevant function. For example, if the succession-planning group has forecast significant opportunity for growth in new markets, additional sales managers are needed. In this case, perhaps only the current marketing or sales managers are asked to nominate high-potential people in their divisions.

Placement of New Hires

When a mentor is to be made available to each new hire, at any level, staff in the hiring and placement functions designate the nominations. Some organizations now offer mentors or buddies to all new hires. Others match mentors only with those expert hires selected to bring in needed technical skills or business acumen.

Whichever strategy you choose, criteria for participating in the process must be made available to every possible source of protégé candidates. Exhibit 9.1 is a sample call for participants using the three relevant strategies.

Exhibit 9.1. Sample Call for Protégé Candidates.

Facilitated Mentoring Process

Candidates are invited to participate in a process to develop specific skills and experiences in a targeted, facilitated interaction with a mentor. To make a nomination:

- Anyone who wishes to participate may nominate himself or herself
- Bosses may nominate subordinates who have the potential to grow and develop additional skills
- Candidates may be nominated by any manager or supervisor who has had experience with assessing the potential of the candidate

Selection Processes

Once a group of potential protégés has been identified, a process of selecting and matching takes place. In today's equal-opportunity environment, training and development programs are supposedly open to all. But strategies for protégé selection can be biased. Problems cited in the selection process (Myers and Humphreys, 1985) include preselection, use of an old-boy network, nepotism, and outright discrimination. For example, when mentors are permitted to nominate protégés, they may secretly select their favorites and then manipulate the matching process to ensure that they get their choice. Or alert protégés may observe the power structure and choose mentors who can give them the best entry into an old-boy network.

In a free-enterprise economy, ownership carries the right to allocate all resources, including development programs. The owners of firms often give favorable treatment to family members and friends. Nepotism has long been an accepted way of building businesses and ensuring continuity of leadership. Many entrepreneurs involve family members in their businesses to get the enterprise off the ground; such favorable treatment becomes troublesome when managers who are not owners practice it. Sometimes executives trade favors with executives in other areas. The vice president of finance asks the vice president of marketing to give a relative a summer job. Or the comptroller asks the chief of personnel to make an internship available for a subordinate of the comptroller.

Discrimination in selecting people for special development programs has hurt women and members of underrepresented groups especially. There are still few women and people of color in high-level, powerful positions. Overtly unfair practices in selecting protégés will result in a discrimination suit. As we saw in Chapter Two, Dr. Margaret Jensvold charged that the National Institute of Mental Health, where she was formerly employed, sexually discriminated against her and that she was also denied the "core benefits of her fellowship" by the institute's "failing to mentor her" (Corbin, 1994). Subtle unfairnesses are difficult to control, yet they can be minimized with a carefully crafted selection process.

How you establish the policy and procedures for selecting and matching protégés to mentors can feed or thwart such undesirable practices. A good example of fair practice can be found at General Electric's Power Generation Division, where mentoring is a vital part of the training for new field engineers (O'Reilly, 1989). Each trainee (GE's term for the protégé) is assigned two mentors. The second one is there to help orient the new engineer if, for whatever reason, the first relationship does not work. Such fail-safe mechanisms can ensure that a protégé receives fair treatment during the developmental process.

I discuss next a few criteria for protégés that you might consider when designing your selection process. All of them help maximize the positive experience for a protégé.

The primary criterion for selection is that the protégé be motivated to develop new competencies or enhance existing ones. No matter how formally or informally the relationship is structured, if the protégé is not motivated, nothing is gained. Facilitated processes work because protégés actively pursue new learning.

The characteristics and responsibilities of participants at RINA Accountancy are described in Exhibit 9.2.

Two other criteria for protégé selection are ability to perform in more than one functional area, and assessed potential to perform at

Exhibit 9.2. Sample of Announced Characteristics of Protégés.

Characteristics and Responsibilities of Participants in the RINA Accountancy Mentoring Program

It is expected that participants in the mentoring program have these characteristics:

- Goal-oriented
- Willing to assume responsibility for one's own growth and development
- Active in seeking challenging assignments and greater responsibility
- Receptive to feedback and coaching

Responsibilities include:

- Identifying developmental needs and setting development goals
- Formulating an action plan for accomplishing goals
- Maintaining individual development plan documentation
- Regularly contacting the coordinator on the progress of the relationship

Source: Rooney, Ida, Nolt and Ahern, Certified Public Accountants. Used with permission.

least two levels above the present position in the organization. Similar criteria must be established for your process, depending on its goals and the target populations.

→ *Look for the curious individual who is demanding more training and new assignments.*

Motivated individuals are also likely to take personal responsibility for their own growth and development. Mentoring removes the responsibility for skill development from the organization and puts it squarely on the shoulders of the individual, where it belongs. There must therefore be great commitment on the part of the protégé to assume responsibility for his or her own development. With the ease of accessing virtual classrooms and online technical courses, many people are continuing their learning process both for present responsibilities and for future growth. The strategy of self-nomination is the one most likely to yield protégé candidates who are willing to take responsibility for their own development. When sponsors initially make the selection, you cannot make this assumption.

→ *Look for a person who initiates a career-development plan and frequently participates in outside workshops and seminars or takes advantage of online learning.*

Making Plans to Meet Developmental Needs

Individual development planning is still rare. Most protégés will require guidelines and help with assessments.

Diagnosing Needs

Development activities are best targeted to specific, diagnosed needs. Diagnosing developmental needs is done through using everything from formal and external diagnostic centers to the protégé's own gut feeling of what she or he wants. One of the best practices for helping an employee to determine developmental needs is that used by Barbara Williams in the Nuclear Regulatory Commission. Williams interviews each candidate using a checklist of potential needs and developmental strategies. This document is then used to find the most appropriate mentor match and create a workable development plan (interview with author, Apr. 13, 2000). In the past, a few organizations used assessment centers, where protégé candidates take part in simulated business activities, in-basket exercises, employee discussion scenarios, and problem-solving cases. The candidates get feedback on their progress and assessment of their specific developmental needs.

In gathering data for this section of the book and in our discussions with people in a variety of organizations, we found few today that use assessment centers, either internal or external. The popularity of formal assessment centers appears to be waning, while use of assessment instruments is growing. This increase may be due to the growing body of research that validates these tools. The instruments also tend to be far less costly and less cumbersome to administer than participation in an assessment center. The work styles assessment tools have proven exceptionally valuable in jump-starting the relationship building of mentor and protégé.

Browse any resource catalogue and you will find dozens of assessment instruments in categories ranging from assessing managerial or leadership style to aptitude assessment. Exhibitors at every professional conference display a wide variety of resources for assessing skills, communication styles, behaviors, personality types, and learning styles. Every day our mail contains brochures about new instruments and assessment tools. You will certainly have no difficulty finding a full selection of these instruments. The difficulty is in narrowing your choices to those that fit your needs and are practical to use in your environment.

Here is a brief description of a few of the assessment instruments that could be used to diagnose developmental needs of protégés in a mentoring process. This list is far from complete and is not meant as an endorsement of these over any other similar instruments. Tools are time savers, and time is always limited for development activities. Make the most of it with appropriate tools and aids. The resource section of this book contains complete information on the publishers of these instruments.

The Personal Profile System, marketed by Inscape Publishing, is a work-behavior assessment profile that can assist the participant in identifying similarities and differences in mentor and protégé work-behavior patterns. It displays the primary tendencies of Dominance, Steadiness, Influencing of Others, and Conscientiousness of the respondent. In addition to the primary tendencies, behaviors are described more precisely for the respondent in graphs illustrating three of the fifteen Classical Profile Patterns.

A similar instrument, I-Sight, also marketed by Inscape Publishing, is a brief assessment of style and is particularly useful for younger people or those with limited English language skills.

With adult-student pairs, the Personal Profile System for the adult and I-Sight for the student gives them language that enhances their communication and avoids what might otherwise become an obstacle in their work together.

Another self-rating process, this one with ten "personal-growth" skills areas, is Managing Personal Growth (Blessing/White). The indicators assessed with this tool are knowing what you want from life; having a realistic sense of personal strengths and weaknesses; making decisions and setting priorities with good judgment; initiating action; generating new ideas and alternative solutions; anticipating and seizing opportunities; planning; getting support from others; learning; and being optimistic, decisive, flexible, purposeful, motivated, enthusiastic, assertive, and confident.

20/20 Insight GOLD (Performance Support Systems) is a software-based 360-degree feedback tool that can produce data for development planning. The software includes wizards, a survey library, measurement scales, comment options, respondent media options, and the individual development plan.

SKILLSCOPE (Center for Creative Leadership) assesses managers' strengths and developmental needs. Ninety-eight skills are assessed in major classes such as information exchange, interpersonal relationships, influence (both taking and accepting), decision making, and use of self. The instrument must be completed by the respondent and five to eight of the respondent's coworkers.

The Personal Skills Map (Nelson and Low, Emotional Learning Systems) is a self-marking, self-scoring instrument that measures eleven career and life-effectiveness skills on fourteen scales: Self-Esteem, Assertion, Interpersonal Comfort, Empathy, Drive Strength, Decision Making, Time Management, Sales Orientation, Commitment Ethic, Stress Management, and Physical Wellness. The respondent's personal communication style is assessed on scales of Interpersonal Assertion, Interpersonal Aggression, and Interpersonal Deference. The degree of satisfaction with current skill levels is assessed on the scale of Personal Change Orientation. This instrument is particularly useful for establishing a baseline of these career effectiveness skills prior to beginning the development program. At an appropriate interval following practice of the skills, it can be taken again to measure and evaluate the degree of change.

→ *Look for tools and processes that fit the need and are valid, reliable, and easy to use for coordinators, mentors, and protégés.*

Preparing an Individual Development Plan

It takes more than a word of encouragement to make the protégé responsible for his or her own development. Protégés must have a development plan based on diagnosed needs and supported by adequate resources.

Before any developmental plan can be completed, however, the amount of time the protégé can dedicate to mentoring activities as opposed to "the real job" must be determined. Mentoring activities may be totally on company time, the protégé's own time, or a combination of the two. In current practice, the time spent in developmental activities is most often in addition to the regular job, for both mentor and protégé. It is encouraging to see some organizations creating mentor and protégé charge codes for time spent in the learning activities. This sends a clear message that growth and development is a priority.

Once the desired skills and experiences are known and how the time is to be handled has been agreed on, the development plan can be drafted. It can be as simple as a few lines on a card that serve as the basis for discussion between the mentor and protégé. It can also be a multipage form that records planned activities for several months or years. Ideally the development plan uses the same format as the one for performance planning, objective setting, and action planning. The documented details include projected outcomes, time lines, resources required, and progress checkpoints. The key is to make it work for the protégé, rather than consuming a lot of effort in maintaining the document.

Exhibit 9.3 is a sample of guidelines for the protégé to use in preparing an initial development plan. Exhibit 9.4 is a sample form for planning and tracking developmental activities. After the initial drafting by the protégé, the document can be refined by all interested parties. In the GAO's Executive Candidate Development Program, the candidate designs an eighteen-month development plan,

Exhibit 9.3. Sample Development Plan Guidelines.

Each goal is recorded on a separate development plan worksheet. Your goals may be professional, educational, and personal. Some examples are marketing results, advancement, staff recruitment, chargeable hours, and development of special skills. The development plan is to be completed by the participant. Spaces are provided for:

Name:	[yours]
Date:	Date by which you expect to have accomplished the goal.
Career goal:	In this space write the goal you wish to achieve. Make the statement in terms of the outcome, or end result, rather than the process you will use to get there.
Development objective:	State the skill, experience, or competency you wish to gain, in measurable terms.
Action steps:	List detailed, sequential steps for how to achieve this objective.
Target dates:	For each action step, enter a target date for completion. Pencil these dates in your daily planner to help stay on schedule.
Resources required:	You may need assistance from someone other than your mentor. List people, places, funds, and any other items you anticipate needing to accomplish each action.
Status and progress comments:	Use this column to prepare for discussion with your mentor and for reinforcing yourself for completing scheduled action steps. Enter comments about the status of each action, progress made since the last review, and so on.
	When appropriate, note concerns that you wish to discuss with your mentor. Enter the date of the discussion.
	Add action steps and additional target dates when appropriate.

Exhibit 9.4. Sample Development Plan Form.

Name: _____

Date: _____

Career goal: _____

Development objective:

Action Steps	Target Dates	Resources Required	Status and Progress Comments

To whom will I communicate accomplishment of this goal? _____

Source: Career Planning Workbook. Copyright © 1995, MMHA The Managers' Mentors, Inc. Used with permission.

which is reviewed by the boss, the mentor, and the Executive Resources Board (see Chapter Six).

Should the immediate manager or team leader be included in approving the development plan? It depends on the organization. In some cases, the natural boss's responsibility is for job and task functions only and does not include career-development planning. In accounting, information technology, and legal firms, staff is assigned to a manager or team leader for a relatively short-term project, engagement, or case. These managers probably have little interest in the long-term career development of the junior members on the team; the focus is on getting the project completed or the case settled. Long-term developmental planning is often the responsibility of a partner or of the personnel administrator. In such a case, the manager is involved in the development plans of team members only if some of the learning activities are to be carried out during the time of the work assignment.

In contrast, most industry assignments at the management level run from two to five years. In this environment, the natural boss is usually aware of the importance of including development plans with other planned objectives. The longer duration of the boss-subordinate relationship in these organizations makes it easy to look for opportunities and projects that result in the protégé learning new skills.

→ *Find or design a simple development plan form that provides a record of skills and experiences to be gained, types of learning activity to be pursued, and an approximate time frame for completing the planned activities.*

Checklist

This chapter gives you some of the how-tos of identifying and selecting protégés, diagnosing developmental needs, and devising development plans. You can prepare for these processes by answering the questions on the checklist in Exhibit 9.5.

Exhibit 9.5. Checklist for Identifying and Selecting Protégés and Making Plans to Meet Their Developmental Needs.

Action to Take

1. What term will we use for the role of protégé?   _____

2. How are candidates for protégés nominated?   _____

3. What criteria do we use to select individuals into the mentoring process?   _____

4. What is the balance of time commitments to the protégé's core job and to development activities?   _____

5. What steps do we take to encourage protégés to take responsibility for their own growth and development?   _____

6. What processes or tools are used to diagnose the developmental needs of the protégé?   _____

7. What format does the development plan have?   _____

8. Who has a part in reviewing the development plan?   _____

9. What can protégés expect, realistically, about promotion?   _____

10. What agreements about the use of the mentor's and protégé's time do we recommend?   _____

11. How do we orient the protégés to their role?   _____

Other questions

12. _____   _____

13. _____   _____

14. _____   _____

Chapter Ten

Involving the Boss
Who Is Not the Mentor

How does the manager or team leader (for ease of distinguishing roles, I call this person the natural boss) of the protégé react to having a subordinate involved in a mentoring relationship? This concern is frequently raised when someone other than the protégé's direct-line supervisor functions as a mentor. Indeed, this triangle can present a number of problems, which I discuss in this chapter along with possible solutions.

Objections Raised by Natural Bosses

The boss who is not good at developing subordinates may not understand the nature of the protégé's development activities. He or she may be suspicious and resentful of the subordinate taking the time to go to a meeting that is seemingly unrelated to the protégé's current assignment, not understanding that the purpose of attending is to observe and learn good techniques for leading meetings. A boss with this perception of mentoring activities is also overlooking the fact that the skill building taking place may benefit the protégé's regular job performance as well.

Jealousy and insecurity are other potential problems. Sometimes, the protégé's mentor is at a higher level in the organization than the boss. Suddenly, the subordinate has access to information and networks that the boss doesn't have. The boss begins to feel inadequate or left out.

Other bosses do not believe in development programs of any sort. Most managers and administrators still feel that getting the immediate job done right is the only priority. A short-term team or engagement leader has the immediate project as the priority. This belief is evidenced by the inevitable cancellation of a planned training course whenever there is any risk of failing to meet production schedules. Bosses who believe that they are letting protégés off for "extra" development assignments view time away from the job as a cost rather than an investment.

Some bosses who are not committed to development programs think that people should have all the required skills and abilities when they take a job. In reality, even in the best of labor situations it is unusual to find the mix of skills necessary to perfectly match the requirements of an open position. In employment boom times—with only 4.2 percent of the workforce considered unemployed (U.S. Department of Labor, 1999)—it is difficult to find those with the skills needed for many jobs.

In addition, some bosses lack commitment specifically to the mentoring process: "I got here through my own hard work and initiative. Why should we give special attention to young employees?"

Overcoming Objections and Gaining Commitment

It is necessary to build into your design some mechanisms to prevent the insecure boss from undermining the process. How do you get agreement and support from the boss? Here are some suggestions.

Plan for Shared Responsibility Between the Mentor and the Boss

The current boss knows how the protégé is performing on the job and can make valuable suggestions for the protégé's development plan, which should include activities for strengthening skills required to perform effectively in the current job as well as for acquiring skills needed for the future. When the agreement is negotiated between the mentor and protégé, the boss can make suggestions and pass on information ahead of time, or be an active participant in the discussion. In a well-designed and facilitated mentoring process, the supervisor participates all along the way.

Input is given at the point of planning development activities, at the initial nomination, during the orientation, and prior to each progress review meeting. In addition, as the boss may have more opportunity to observe the protégé's day-to-day performance than the mentor does, it follows that the boss has more opportunities to provide feedback and coaching. By being a part of the process in these ways, the boss takes a stake in the protégé's success and becomes an interested party, committed to the process.

If the boss is in the best position to know and observe the protégé, why shouldn't the boss be the formal mentor? In a sense, all bosses should be doing *informal* mentoring of their subordinates for the skills required for the particular job. However, the goal of most mentoring processes is to broaden the skills of the protégé. I have said previously that an advantage of having a mentor from another function is that it brings to the protégé a new perspective. In one health care environment (Brockbank and Beech, 1999), research showed that bosses who took on the role of mentor were not comfortable in the dual role: "The four [pairs] whom we tracked in depth were also the line managers of their mentees, which accentuated their role as assessors and heightened this conflict" (p. 53). Finally, not all bosses have the skills that good mentors need. Most organizations still do not adequately prepare those who are promoted to supervisory or management positions.

→ *Structure the development plan to allow both boss and mentor input.*

Plan for Interaction Between the Boss and the Mentor

This planned interaction can reduce the boss's concern about the protégé's being involved in a special relationship with another, perhaps higher-level, manager. At Merrill Lynch (Farren, Gray, and Kaye, 1984) the mentor is encouraged to call each protégé's manager and get acquainted. The mentor works with four protégés during a six-month period, and both the mentor and the protégés keep the managers apprised of what they're doing.

The coordination team may also convene periodic meetings of the boss, mentor, and protégé to discuss the progress of the development plan. If periodic meetings are typically scheduled with mentors only, the bosses can be included occasionally. It would be relatively easy to design some exercises for those meetings to guide the boss and mentor in a discussion of the protégé's progress and further developmental needs.

One word of caution. When the mentor and boss are interacting regularly, the protégé may be uncomfortable discussing confidential issues with the mentor, particularly if they concern issues or problems that involve the boss. The mentor must be prepared to keep the protégé's trust and deal with such private information diplomatically and sensitively.

➔ *Look for ways to bring the boss, mentor, and protégé together regularly.*

Communicate to the Boss How the Subordinate Will Benefit

Initial anxiety and fear of losing control may obscure an important benefit for the boss. The boss's job can be made easier when the protégé is taking full responsibility for the tasks of preparing and executing a development plan. Further, as the protégé is given positive feedback for carrying out these tasks, they transfer to the day-to-day job. An alert boss can reinforce this behavior by commending the employee for taking the initiative in performance planning and tracking progress.

Let the boss know about such benefits in the material you use to promote the process. Stress the fact that the protégé's development plan can be tied to regular performance plans. The coordination team can also tell bosses of such benefits during the protégé nomination and selection process.

➔ *Communicate to the boss the benefits of having a subordinate who is in a mentoring relationship.*

Alert the Boss to Opportunities to Learn About People Development

The boss who is not a world-class supervisor has an opportunity to learn valuable skills for managing people by observing how a competent mentor interacts with a protégé. While never having to admit the lack of those particular skills, the boss can watch them modeled by the mentor and then imitate them in performance planning and feedback discussions with the protégé and other subordinates. In an experience exchange focus group, a mentor said, "I'm handling management of my direct reports in fourteen countries much better by applying the strategies my mentee and I worked out for successful feedback and coaching when we were eight thousand miles apart" (conversation with the author, 1998).

➔ *Alert the boss to opportunities to learn from the mentor.*

Use the Process to Make the Boss Aware of the Benefits of Human Resource Development

Line managers are often skeptical of the value of development activities. They see human resources as a costly staff function that has questionable results. With facilitated mentoring, the process coordination team has an opportunity to consult with the boss and get support for all development processes. I saw an e-mail message from one manager expressing profound appreciation to a mentor for helping the protégé grow in a way that literally saved him from being terminated.

The mentoring process should be presented as one component of the total program rather than as a separate function. Ideally, as a result, the boss becomes a stakeholder in all development functions. Instead of being an adversary, the boss sees the whole program as a potential resource for development of all subordinates.

➔ *Look for a way to build bridges between the boss, the mentor, and the human resource staff.*

Checklist

What other ideas do you have for strategies for involving the boss of a protégé? Use the checklist in Exhibit 10.1 to come up with your own action items.

Exhibit 10.1. Checklist for Involving the Natural Boss.

Action to Take

1. How does the natural boss give input to the protégé's development plan?

2. How does the natural boss become involved with the mentor?

3. What do we do to gain commitment from the natural boss?

4. How does the protégé build development activities into the regular job?

5. How can we encourage the natural boss to learn from the mentor?

6. How can the coordinator build the boss's confidence in human resource programs and the mentoring process?

Other questions

7. _____

8. _____

9. _____

Chapter Eleven

The Coordination Team

Selection, Training, and Responsibilities

Competent coordination is central to the success of facilitated mentoring. The coordination team members orchestrate all the elements of the process. In most instances, the coordination team members are permanent employees, usually with other duties in operations, finance, human resources, or personnel. Small organizations, or those with small pilot processes, might consider contracting this function out. It is often more cost-effective to outsource tasks that do not fall within the core business.

With mentoring processes in educational institutions or targeted to youth in a certain community, the coordination team typically has a representative from each of the stakeholder groups—students or youths, teachers, counselors, parents or guardians, mentors, and employers.

First of all, the coordination team scans the environment to determine what needs, goals, and opportunities are visible that suggest doing something different about developing targeted groups of people. They then assist in selecting, assessing, matching, and orientating mentors and protégés. Additional responsibilities can be assigned to the coordination team depending on the nature and structure of the process. Essentially, the coordination team members are relationship managers who see that the needs of the mentor, protégé, and organization are met. Often overlooked tasks of the coordination team are those of tracking, monitoring, and evaluating the results of the process. This chapter includes specific guidelines for structuring the coordination team role.

Selection

Before you begin to think about the mechanics of coordination, it is useful to review the reasons why you want a facilitated mentoring process in the first place. If you are in a corporate setting, your organization more than likely has specific succession-planning goals. You want to have enough people ready now to fill all projected staffing requirements. You are looking for more than just warm bodies; you want people with relevant skills for each projected position. You are probably not going to locate and hire people who already have the requisite skills, so you must facilitate the growth and development of the organization's people. Your decision may be to structure a mentoring process to meet this goal.

If your organization has placed a high priority on the mentoring process, the next major decision is whom to select as members of the coordination team. The multifaceted role of the coordination team is a most critical one for a facilitated mentoring process. Don't put a junior person with minimal skills in a coordination team role.

In a corporate environment, the coordination team must have up-to-date knowledge of the business plan and all supporting strategic plans. In a government agency, the coordination team needs to know, at the least, the projections for staff and the anticipated budget for training and development. In a nonprofit group, the coordination team might need to know the numbers and ratios of paid professionals and volunteers on the staff. Even more important, the coordination team in any organization must have the respect and cooperation of the top people. Without this respect, and considerable skills, it is impossible for the team to mediate sensitive discussions and resolve them effectively.

It is also useful to create a hierarchy of the skills required on the coordination team after the role and tasks have been defined. This template can facilitate finding the most appropriate persons for the team and eventually certifying their competence if that is desirable.

You must also look at how many coordination team members your process needs. To some extent, the total number of people in the organization may determine this number; it is influenced by how many people are involved in mentor-protégé relationships at any given time. If a process is small, this function can be handled in addition to other human resource responsibilities, such as recruitment, placement, training, and development. It is risky to overload a coordination team, however. The team must be able to give high priority to preventing potential problems and resolving those problems that do come up. Exhibit 11.1 describes the role of the coordination team in a small organization. Use the description to gauge the number of team members your process needs.

Exhibit 11.1. Sample Coordination Team Responsibilities.

The basic responsibility of the mentoring process coordination team is to facilitate the successful growth of people in the organization. The coordination team is a primary resource to protégés and mentors and may be contacted with any questions about the mentoring process. Here are brief descriptions of the specific functions of the coordination team.

Planning and designing the process	The goals, needs, and opportunities facing the organization establish the need the mentoring process must fill. The purpose, goals, and desired outcomes for the process must be carefully documented to gain and sustain support for it.
Creating and executing a communication plan	A comprehensive communication plan that targets each group having a need to know ideally includes a time line that prompts issuance of timely information.
Maintaining mentor pool	The goal is to have an adequate pool of mentors to make appropriate and timely matches with protégés. The coordination team periodically requests volunteers, invites protégés to nominate their preferences of mentors, and receives recommendations from managers and other leaders.

1. Recruiting
    A. A call for nominations is extended periodically. Protégés nominate candidates as potential mentors.
    B. As needed, the coordination team requests volunteers and ask for recommendations from managers and other leaders.

(Continued)

Exhibit 11.1. Sample Coordination Team Responsibilities, Continued.

        C. Volunteers may advise the coordination team of interest and availability at any time. For example, a new hire with particular expertise may volunteer to be a mentor.

    2. Screen and match

        A. A database of mentor-protégé relationships is maintained.

        B. The coordination team interacts with department heads and firm leaders to determine the most appropriate match of mentors and protégés.

        C. The coordination team may be contacted by either the mentor or the protégé to develop a new match (for example, the protégé attains all goals set with the current mentor and wishes to develop in another area).

Assisting with development goals	Regularly assess areas for growth and development of potential protégés.

    1. Review personnel files for indicators of particular strengths and needs.

    2. Review recent self-evaluations.

    3. Analyze recent assessments of skills, behaviors, and styles.

Negotiating the agreement	Typically, the mentor and protégé negotiate the specifics of their agreement. Members of the coordination team are available to participate in the discussion when appropriate. The coordination team provides possible agreement and development-plan formats.
Conducting meetings	The coordination team conducts group meetings of mentors and protégés when appropriate to facilitate experience exchange and collect data for the evaluation.
Conducting mentor orientation	The coordination team conducts mentor orientations according to guidelines provided.
Conducting protégé orientation	The coordination team conducts protégé orientations according to guidelines.
Maintaining records	Involvement in the program is noted in mentor and protégé personnel files.

Just as with any other key position in the organization, it is important to create a succession plan for the coordination team. Sustaining the process with continuity of participation and fidelity to the design prevents a potential pitfall of having it be seen as a fad or *programme du jour*.

Responsibilities

This point-by-point discussion of coordination team responsibilities helps those of you who are selecting coordination team members and those coordination team members who want to get a good grasp of their responsibilities.

Facilitating Growth of Protégés

As with mentors, a primary consideration is to find coordination team members who care about the growth and development of others because most of their time is spent looking out for someone else's needs. They must be good listeners who can judge a person's motivation level and personal needs. They must also be quick to sense problems that surface during the mentoring relationship. Often such problems are unspoken—they are manifested in a protégé's body language or in unreturned phone calls to the mentor. Coordination team members must be able to pick up such cues, analyze them, and act quickly. To do so, they must be skilled in all of the following areas:

- Coaching
- Counseling
- Communicating with appropriate assertiveness
- Negotiating
- Giving feedback

The coordination team members act as coaches to all parties in the mentoring process, from initial screening of mentors to dissolution of the relationship. Many situations call for coaching. For example, the coordination team members may coach both the mentor and the protégé in preparing to negotiate their agreement. They may also coach the bosses in how to appropriately interact with mentors and protégés.

In addition, finely honed counseling skills are necessary in both routine and unusual circumstances. The coordination team members must be equally prepared to counsel the protégé who is frustrated with a career and the one who confesses a sexual attraction to the mentor.

Appropriately assertive communication skills are useful to the coordination team members in such situations—and critical when an issue in the relationship has escalated to the point where the coordination team is sought out to resolve it. Similarly, negotiation skills are called for in every activity, from building an initial, hopeful agreement to terminating a disappointing one.

Good feedback skills are a must for coordination team members. The ability to recognize what type of feedback is relevant to each person and in each situation, and to give feedback that reinforces desired behavior, is one of the most valuable skills for keeping mentoring relationships on the positive side.

→ *Look for a diplomat to fill the coordination team member role.*

Analyzing Jobs, Tasks, and Needs

Coordination team members must also have good, practical analysis skills. For starters, they must be able to analyze jobs and tasks and determine what kind of ability and experience a position requires. Assessment of the protégé's developmental needs is another key skill for coordination team members. If you plan to use any developmental diagnostic instruments, such as those for assessing skills, patterns of work behaviors, or personality, the coordination team members must have extensive background in the theoretical research on and application of such instruments. Training and practice in administering and interpreting the selected tools is an essential part of preparing coordination team members for their role.

→ *Look for a coordination team member with a background in research and performance technology.*

Promoting the Process

The coordination team must be able to design and develop exciting promotional materials to attract participants. At the same time, these materials must present the process specifics accurately so that only qualified participants apply. This is the challenge for a good public-relations writer.

→ *Look for a person skillful at writing and marketing.*

Coordinating Multiple Activities

The coordination team administers all elements of the mentoring process. Some nitty-gritty record keeping is involved, as well as the fascinating aspects of being in on advance planning for the organization. The models in Chapter Six illustrate the many components of various types of programs. At a minimum, the coordination team is in charge of the following:

- Setting process goals
- Identifying protégés
- Screening mentor-candidates
- Matching mentors with protégés
- Conducting orientation programs
- Negotiating agreements
- Tracking the health of the relationships
- Evaluating the effectiveness of the process

→ *Look for people with strong administrative skills.*

Gaining and Maintaining the Commitment of Top Management

Occasionally, the process may come under scrutiny or suffer when top management forgets to make it a priority. If emotions run high, the coordination team must have sufficient clout to work priority and budget issues with top managers. The team must also be able to keep the process visible.

➔ *Give the coordination team authority and status.*

Working with an Advisory Board

It may be advantageous to select an advisory board made up of representatives from every function in the organization to create policy and to give guidance to the process coordination team. If the leaders of all functions are held responsible for the process, support is built in from the beginning. A panel or group of advisers brings a broad range of knowledge about the future direction of the organization and is an excellent source of information about future job opportunities.

Such a board exists in the GAO's Executive Candidate Development Program (ECDP), as illustrated in Chapter Six: "The Executive Resources Board (ERB) is responsible for the structure, content, and operation of the program, inclusive of assessing needs for executives, initiating new ECDP classes and making recommendations concerning which senior level managers should be selected into the program" (Glazer and Murray, 1990). The ERB is directly involved in all aspects of the program, with these tasks and responsibilities:

- Approves mentors for each of the candidates (protégés)
- Reviews and approves each candidate's proposed development plan
- Monitors and assesses each candidate's progress and performance throughout the length of the process
- Advises candidates on suggested changes to the development plan

- Makes a judgment on program certification
- Makes a placement decision at the conclusion of the program
- Makes a decision about program structure and content

Coordination team members must be able to use advisory boards for support and useful advice. They must be willing to share the responsibility and to make visible use of the evaluations and recommendations that the board makes.

→ *Select a coordination team member who accepts and uses feedback.*

Matching Mentor and Protégé

Earlier chapters described the need to carefully match protégés and mentors using objective criteria based on the protégés' developmental needs and the ability of the mentors to act as resources for fulfilling those needs. At every step of the way, the coordination team must be sure that roles are clear and that the match is appropriate. For an open process in a fairly large organization, here is a list of the tasks of the coordination team in matching and preparing the mentor and protégé for their mentoring relationship:

1. The lead coordinator for a mentor-protégé pair is one with an established relationship with the mentor. Another coordination team member is an alternate contact.
2. The coordination team member contacts the mentor to advise of potential selection.
3. Coordination team member and mentor candidate meet to

   Describe the facilitated mentoring process

   Assess commitment of mentor candidate

   Gain indication of match to protégé
4. Notify matched mentor and other potential mentors of the status of their selection.

5. Meet with selected mentor individually to

    Brief on protégé biography

    Assign orientation prework if appropriate: Personal Skills Map, Personal Profile System

    Schedule orientation for mentor

6. Meet with protégé individually to

    Brief on mentor biography

    Assign orientation prework if appropriate: Personal Skills Map, Personal Profile System

    Schedule orientation for protégé

7. Notify the bosses of both partners of the proposed match. The mentor and protégé may do this themselves.

➜ *Look for a coordination team member who pays attention to detail.*

Designing Orientations

How the mentors and protégés are prepared for their roles and responsibilities directly influences how they relate to each other and how they carry out the development activities. The coordination team usually has the responsibility of designing the orientation to fit the policies and structure of the specific process. The coordination team has to be astute at assessing the best way to meet the needs of mentors and protégés. For example, when you start your process it may be most effective to conduct a group orientation for all mentors. As the process continues and additional people assume the mentor role, it may be convenient for the coordination team to do individual orientations. Another option is to have a top-notch mentor orient the new one, a sort of peer mentoring.

Similarly, the orientation for protégés who are already employed but new to a mentoring relationship differs from that for those new employees who go directly into a mentoring relationship. Once you have an established mentoring process that is available to everyone, the regular orientation to the organization and the job can include the features and responsibilities of the mentoring relationships. At the least, the coordination team must structure orientations and find the appropriate people to conduct them. The members may facilitate the orientations or contract this infrequent task to a skilled facilitator. Exhibits 11.2 and 11.3 illustrate the types of activity that might take place in mentor and protégé group orientations. Exhibit 11.4 is the outline for an individual orientation of protégés in an open-to-all mentoring program at a small firm.

Exhibit 11.2. Sample Outline for Group Orientation of Mentors.

Activity	Process and Resources
Self-assessment of generic career and life skills	Personal Skills Map (PSM)
Recognizing human motivation needs	Presentation
Researching mission, values, and culture of organization	Group process
Mentoring process as component of human resource development, staffing requirements, and succession plans	Presentation
Roles of the four parties in the facilitated mentoring process	Presentation and discussion
Identifying individual work behavior patterns (if not done as prework)	Personal Profile System (PPS)
Documenting personal values, needs, and interests	Guided individual process
Assessment of skills against criteria for mentors	Mentor and PSM interpretation
Elements of workable agreements	Presentation
Setting project reporting requirements with process coordination team	Discussion
Feedback principles and techniques (feedback and coaching skills)	Self-study or workshop
Other skill development needed:	
How to get started (for example, using PPS)	Guidelines
Negotiating agreement with protégé	Application
Assist protégé with inventory of qualifications for target jobs	Application
Drafting individual development plans	Application with protégé

Exhibit 11.3. Sample Outline for Group Orientation of Protégés.

Activity	Process and Resources
Complete biographical data sheet	Individual
Self-assessment of generic career and life skills (if not done as prework)	Personal Skills Map (PSM)
Recognizing human motivation needs	Presentation
Researching mission, values, and culture of organization	Group process
Roles of the four parties in the facilitated mentoring process	Presentation and discussion
Identifying individual work behavior patterns (if not done as prework)	Personal Profile System (PPS)
Documenting personal values, needs, and interests (individual development plan)	Guided individual process
Managing personal growth (optional)	Workshop or 20/20 Insight GOLD (optional)
Finding a mentor and negotiating workable agreements	Presentation
Setting project reporting requirements	Discussion with coordinator
Drafting career goals and job targets	Individual work
Making an inventory of qualifications	Application
Negotiating agreement with mentor	Application
Developing individual development plan	Application with mentor

Exhibit 11.4. Sample Outline for Individual Orientation of Participants.

Outcomes	*Activity and Resources*
The firm:	Coordination team
• Mission, goals, and projected growth	
• How the mentoring process supports the mission and goals	Philosophy statement
Policies:	Coordination team
• What the mentoring process is and isn't	Structure for the process
• Where the present job can lead; career paths	Staff manual
• What development activities are available within the firm	
• Resources that are available for external education and development activities	
• Time and expense reporting when in mentoring activities	
• Mentoring process involvement	
Establishing the mentor relationship:	Coordination team
• Initial match	
• How to get the next one	
Negotiating the agreement:	Coordination team
• Confidentiality	
• Duration of the relationship	
• Suggested format	Agreement format
• Elements of the discussion	Examples provided
• No-fault conclusion	
Development plan:	Coordination team
• Suggested format	Development plan
• Setting goals for development	
• Creating action plans	Samples provided
• Reporting progress to mentor, personnel administration (six months)	
Examples of mentor activities:	Coordination team
• Meetings with participant for coaching or training	

(Continued)

Exhibit 11.4. Sample Outline for Individual Orientation of Participants, Continued.

Outcomes	*Activity and Resources*
• Observing participant activities and giving feedback later	
• Recommendations for developmental assignments, training, and so on	
• How the mentor and the engagement supervisor(s) or boss interact	
Recognition for mentors:	Coordination team
• Participants who have a particularly good example of a mentor activity relay the example to the coordination team for recognition of the mentor.	
Coordination team role:	Coordination team
• Matching mentor-participant pairs	
• Maintaining matrix of active relationships	
• Monitoring progress of development with the participant	
• Reporting to firm's partners on progress of mentoring process	
• Resource for counsel on issues	
• Conclusion of relationships	
• Chairing experience meetings with mentors	
• Chairing experience meetings with participants	

Source: Rooney, Ida, Nolt and Ahern, Certified Public Accountants. Used with permission.

➔ *Look for a coordination team member who has experience in structuring and facilitating group activities.*

Tracking the Health of Relationships

A significant part of the coordination responsibility is monitoring relationships and seeing that they remain healthy and productive. This tracking can be accomplished in a variety of ways. To reinforce the flexibility of the process and the responsibility of the protégé for his or her own development, the protégé may report progress primarily to the coordination team. A report need not be detailed and formally documented. It might be as simple as an "all is well" telephone call or electronic message once a quarter or each month.

In addition, the protégé may send a copy of the individual development goals and action plans to the coordination team every month or two. Progress could be noted, along with any difficulties. In the orientation outline shown in Exhibit 11.4, the protégé reports such progress to the coordination team at six-month intervals.

The coordination team may regularly convene meetings of all or some of the mentors in active relationships, perhaps every other month. The protégés can also meet as a group on the alternate month. When it seems appropriate to reconsider the structure and policies of the process, mentors, protégés, and bosses may meet for an open discussion of experiences. All these techniques can help to keep relationships healthy and vital. This attention to continuous quality improvement of the process also communicates that the leaders consider ongoing learning and development a priority.

→ *The coordination team must see the relationship as an ongoing, changeable organism that is constantly monitored.*

Checklist

As you can see, the tasks of team coordination must go to skillful, multitalented persons. The most effective team members keep their skills honed and seek innovation in their process. A good succession plan maintains the vitality and currency of the team. Use Exhibit 11.5 (on next page) to help structure this role.

Exhibit 11.5. Checklist for Structuring the Role of Coordinators.

Action to Take

1. Where do we place the coordination function? _____

2. What is the level of the coordinator(s)? _____

3. How do we assess the skills of coordination team members? _____

4. What training is made available to the coordination team members? _____

5. What program-management responsibilities does the coordination team have? _____

6. What resources are made available for coordination? _____

7. Who is on the advisory board for the coordination team? _____

8. What types of reporting and tracking do we want? _____

Other questions

9. _____   _____

10. _____   _____

Chapter Twelve

Negotiating Sound Mentoring Agreements

After the mentor and protégé have been matched, it is essential to prepare them for a sound, productive relationship. Almost all the questions or complaints I have heard from a mentoring pair could have been prevented by having a clear agreement. Once the basic development objectives have been determined, the mentor and protégé must negotiate an agreement for their partnership.

The success of the mentoring relationship is determined to a great extent by the clarity and reasonableness of this agreement. It does not matter whether it is a typed form or written on the back of an old envelope, or not written at all. The discussion must be clear and complete. Most of the issues that surface during mentoring relationships can be prevented with frank discussions at the outset. This chapter has suggestions for the key components of an agreement and guidelines for putting the agreement together.

In business organizations, the ideal mentoring agreement is jointly agreed to by protégé, mentor, coordination team member, and, if appropriate, the natural boss. In nonprofit organizations or educational institutions, the agreement discussion may take place between protégé and mentor only. Each party brings a set of expectations to the negotiating table. Each may also bring some anxieties and fears. The protégé may expect to improve skills, gain political savvy, and increase the chances of being promoted. The mentor in almost any environment expects to be respected, renewed, admired, and perhaps to get an extra head and pair of hands to carry out work tasks. The natural boss probably has the least specific expectations, unless the process is a mature one with clearly stated criteria and procedures. The boss who is new to the mentoring process may expect more interference than assistance from the mentor. At a minimum, the agreement must express the outcomes wanted by all three parties. The coordinator is there to see that everyone's interests are served within the goals and objectives of the process.

Basic Guidelines

The articles of indenture of medieval times specified the rights and duties of both the master and the apprentice (Eby and Arrowood, 1940). The master sponsored and cared for the apprentice, and in turn the apprentice agreed to guard the master's interests. These agreements went far beyond our current notions of a typical mentor-protégé, employer-employee, or teacher-student relationship. However, two elements need to be specified in any mentoring agreement: the role of the mentor and the goals of the protégé.

Specific Role of the Mentor

The basic nature of the mentoring relationship must be discussed and expressed in the agreement. Some relationships are quite loosely structured. For example, the role of the mentor may be merely to serve as a role model for the protégé; the mentor may be expected simply to invite the protégé to observe handling of certain activities and events in the usual flow of the mentor's job. Time may be scheduled to discuss the observations and answer the protégé's questions following the observation. On the flip side, the mentor may agree to act as an observer as the protégé carries out some task or activity. Presumably, time is scheduled afterwards for feedback and perhaps for coaching to improve future learning and performance.

To go a step further on the involvement scale, a mentor may serve as a guide in preparing the protégé for a specific responsibility or task. The mentor may model the desired behaviors, demonstrate, or coach the protégé. The protégé can also be assigned projects that produce a desired result.

If the mentor's role is established ahead of time, both the protégé and mentor have realistic expectations, and the mentor is not tempted to overextend time commitments.

➔ *Establish the role of the mentor first, to focus the agreement.*

Protégé's Goals

The protégé should bring a draft of the development plan to the first meeting with the mentor and coordinator. The plan may be prepared in collaboration with the boss, it may be drafted by the protégé alone, or it may be drafted in the orientation session. It should contain career goals and development objectives that the protégé wants to focus on. This document is the foundation of the agreement and determines the type of relationship that ensues.

The negotiated agreement should specify how the development plan is to be carried out through mentoring activities. If the mentor and protégé agree to work on only specific skill development, it is relatively easy to describe the activities. It is harder to describe activities for other expectations, such as learning cultural values, making political contacts, and increasing know-how. Unclear or unrealistic expectations are an invitation to disaster for the relationship—and perhaps even for the reputation of one participant or both. For this reason, expectations must be expressed in concrete terms. The protégé can say, for example, "My goal is to improve my image in the organization. I'm good at what I do, but my relationship with my coworkers is not great. I want you to help me improve my communication skills." The mentor can then agree to suggest training classes, give honest feedback, or model a successful interaction with others. There is no promise that the protégé will improve, only the promise that the mentor will offer ways for that improvement to happen. After all, a mentor can expose a protégé to the organization's political network through introductions and inside knowledge. But there is no way the mentor can guarantee that the protégé can tap into or be welcome in the political network.

➜ *Tie expectations and goals to skills and specific activities.*

Exhibit 12.1 is an example of how to link expectations to specific activities in the negotiated agreement.

Exhibit 12.1. Sample Worksheet for Individual Development Planning.

Expectations	What Protégé Can Do	What Mentor Can Do
Organizational involvement at higher levels	Presentation to staff Learn more about logistics	Invite protégé to executive meetings Use protégé as resource
Chance to have new ideas heard	Seek opportunity for input	Use protégé as sounding board and act as sounding board for protégé's ideas
		Assignments (projects, task forces)
		Consider opportunities for protégé to contribute
Improve personal style	Be open to feedback	Give protégé honest feedback
	Work to improve weaknesses	Suggest training, role models, and so on

Specific Components

In addition to the two basic components just discussed, a mentoring agreement may include some or all of a set of clauses.

Confidentiality Parameters

It is important for the protégé and mentor to trust each other, but both must be comfortable with the kind of information they share. For example, if the protégé confides to the mentor that a coworker has a drug problem, the mentor may be obligated by company policy to take action. Likewise, the protégé who attends an upper-level meeting may not want the burden of knowing ahead of time which coworkers will be laid off.

It is best to establish at the outset the confidentiality parameters. The mentor might want to say that all information shared by the protégé is confidential; or the mentor might want to hear only information that is pertinent to the development plan. If during the relationship a sensitive issue is discussed and an agreement of confidentiality has been made, it must be honored under reasonable circumstances.

→ *Discuss how sensitive issues will be handled.*

Duration of Relationship

Agreeing to the approximate duration of the relationship up front serves two useful purposes. First, it can be motivating. In fact, setting the conclusion time a little short of what might normally be expected is desirable. A looming date for concluding the formal relationship instills a sense of urgency in both mentor and protégé to make the development activities rigorous. The action plan takes on real meaning when events are scheduled fairly tightly. Second, establishing an ending date also reinforces the temporary nature of the relationship, which helps to prevent dependence and possessive behavior from either party.

The development goals and plans for the protégé should be used to establish the duration of the relationship at the beginning. Progress toward accomplishing those agreed goals and the wishes of both parties can drive renegotiating the date if appropriate.

→ *Set a realistic and flexible stopping date.*

No-Fault Termination

The agreement should specify intervals for examining the relationship. At some point, both parties must ask the question, Is it still worth it? If the answer is no, they both must have the option of getting out of the agreement.

Deciding how a soured relationship is concluded before it begins is something like putting together a prenuptial contract. The topic of dissolution may take some of the romance out of the prospective relationship, yet it reduces the likelihood of bitter disagreement later on. The agreement should specify that either party has the option of discontinuing the relationship for any reason, expressed or not. Either may choose to consult the coordinator on how to terminate the agreement gracefully without finding or acknowledging fault.

→ *Discuss the no-fault conclusion.*

Frequency and Type of Meetings

"How often will we meet?" This is a reasonable question to ask, and again it depends to a great extent on the development activities planned. If the development involves chairing a task force to study an issue or problem, the mentor and protégé may meet only once or twice over a period of months, unless something goes wrong. If the type of development desired is general and the activities fairly unstructured, meetings may be scheduled once or twice a month, perhaps during a meal. In contrast, if the mentor is to coach, observe, and give feedback to the protégé for several specific tasks, meetings will be more frequent.

The type of meeting is the next decision to tackle. Is it to be a face-to-face meeting, talking on the telephone, or corresponding electronically? Any of these can be effective. Phone calls and electronic messages take some of the headaches and complications out of meeting if the mentor and protégé are located at a distance from each other.

Lack of availability of the mentor when guidance is wanted or needed can be a great disappointment for the protégé. Yet many protégés are reluctant to demand time from a busy mentor. This issue must be discussed during the negotiation of the agreement.

The mentor can make a statement such as, "If I start neglecting you, call me on the carpet for it. It's your responsibility to help me keep this agreement, too." In addition, the coordinator might agree to track the meetings and take action if they are not frequent enough for the protégé's needs.

→ *Consider the specific activities to be accomplished and ease of contact when establishing meeting times and types.*

Guarantees of Promotion

Some protégés might assume that participating in a mentoring process automatically guarantees eventual promotion. If there is no guarantee, spell it out in the negotiated agreement. In some programs, a successful candidate can expect promotion. In the GAO's Executive Candidate Development Program, recommendation for promotion to executive level is based on successfully executing the development plan and the recommendations of the supervisor and mentor. Program participants know these requirements ahead of time and are realistic about what the process can mean to them.

→ *Clearly state the guarantees, if any.*

Agreement Form

Some organizations require that the mentoring agreement be documented on a standard form. Others require no documentation at all, although for best results, some notes should be made about the agreement and its parameters.

→ *Prepare suggested agreement forms.*

Exhibit 12.2 is one type of form that may be used for documenting the negotiated mentoring agreement.

Exhibit 12.2. Sample Mentoring Agreement Form.

Mentor and Participant Agreement

We are voluntarily entering into a mentoring relationship that we expect to benefit both of us and the firm. We want this to be a rich, rewarding experience, with most of our time together spent in substantive development activities. To minimize the administrative details, we have noted these features of our relationship:

• Confidentiality _____

_____

• Duration of the relationship _____

_____

• Frequency of meetings _____

_____

• Approximate amount of time to be invested by mentor _____

_____

• Specific role of the mentor (model, guide, observe and give feedback, recommend developmental activities, facilitate learning, suggest or offer resources, and so on) _____

_____

• Additional points _____

_____

☐   We have discussed the mentoring experience as a further developmental opportunity and its relationship to the policies and procedures of the firm.

☐   The skill areas to be the focus of the current development period are noted on the individual development plan maintained by the participant.

☐   We agree to a *no-fault* conclusion of this relationship if, for any reason, it seems appropriate.

_____   _____
Mentor   Participant

_____   _____
Date   Date

Source: Rooney, Ida, Nolt and Ahern, Certified Public Accountants. Used with permission.

Checklist

Having a clear agreement saves lots of headaches for everyone involved. It is easier to edit than it is to create, so you will save time for mentors and protégés by giving them suggestions for negotiating their agreements. Finally, give the participants a checklist of points to discuss. It not only makes the discussion efficient but also creates a safe climate for the talk. The checklist in Exhibit 12.3 gives you an opportunity to prepare for negotiating agreements in your facilitated process.

Exhibit 12.3. Checklist for Negotiating Mentoring Agreements.

Action to Take

1. What kinds of role are mentors expected to take? _____ _____

2. How do we deal with issues of confidentiality? _____ _____

3. Who is involved in discussing and negotiating the agreement? _____ _____

4. What duration of the relationship is suggested, if any? _____ _____

5. How is development time reported for the protégé? For the mentor? _____ _____

6. How can the agreement be concluded, if at other than the specified time? _____ _____ _____

Other questions

7. _____ _____
_____ _____

8. _____ _____
_____ _____

Chapter Thirteen

Evaluating Mentoring Process Effectiveness

In Part Two of this book, you have been reading about strategies to make a facilitated mentoring process work in your organization. Knowing whether you are getting what you want from these strategies means having some process for tracking and analyzing the results. In Chapter Seven, you examined several techniques for determining organizational readiness for a facilitated mentoring process. Some of those same strategies yield information about the kind of results you want to be able to look at and assess with an evaluation. For example, you may wish to determine the impact of the mentoring experience on the rate of promotion of the participants, on their skill acquisition, or on the costs of grooming leaders.

The initial enthusiasm for designing a facilitated mentoring process may obscure the importance of measuring the effectiveness of the process. If you think you may want to evaluate it at some future time, it is best to design the process as you formulate its components. If you wait to collect opinions and to measure performance until after the process has been initiated, you will have contaminated data: "To ensure long term senior management support, a mentoring program must have a clear, focused goal and associated metrics" (Blake, 1999, p. 3).

Many examples of the importance of evaluation exist in education, especially when the results of evaluations lead to approval of grant proposals. Although the funding for your facilitated mentoring process may not depend on an evaluation of its efficacy, such an evaluation can help to justify continuation of the process during lean times.

It is encouraging to see a few examples of rigorous evaluation of the mentoring process now in publication. Linda Kyle Stromei conducted a study at Sandia National Laboratories using both quantitative and qualitative data collection methods. Her doctoral dissertation, "An Evaluation of the Effectiveness of a Formal Mentoring Program for Managers and the Determinants of Protégé Satisfaction" (1998), reports her findings. Methods of analysis included descriptive statistics, correlations, t-test, ANOVAs, and regressions. The study revealed that "the results of mentoring can be assessed in a short period of time, when establishing a baseline of skills, conducting a treatment, and testing after the treatment. The protégés showed significant improvement on their leadership effectiveness and flexibility scores" (Stromei, 1999, p. 4).

In a study funded by a grant from the Department of Tourism, Small Business, and Industry in Queensland, Australia, researchers detail the findings on women in management positions and their experiences with mentoring relationships (Limerick, Heywood, and Daws, 1994). They report women with mentors were more aware of the benefits, and the constraints, of such a career-supportive relationship. The authors caution about the potential problems of introducing formal mentoring programs, and they advise that the strategy be integrated as part of a change program, requiring strong support and commitment from senior managers.

This chapter outlines some basic evaluation concepts and techniques. Strategies that are most relevant to assessing the impact of a mentoring process are described. If you feel inclined to throw up your hands and say, "I don't want to deal with all that! All I want to know is, does this program do anything for my people?" skip to the checklist at the end of the chapter to get an overview of the essential elements of an evaluation.

Key Terms and Concepts

Decision makers are concerned mostly with the value, effectiveness, costs, cost benefits, and cost-effectiveness of new programs

(Orlansky, 1989). Methods for examining these outcomes have been fairly well established for functions other than human resource development. It is time the available research on evaluation was applied rigorously to training and development.

Costs

Costs are the resources, expressed in monetary terms, needed by a process to accomplish a desired result. Examples of resources needed for training are course materials, equipment and facilities, and students' and instructors' time. All processes consume resources. Resources assigned to one process are no longer available for others. Assigning funds to a particular process is, in effect, a decision to pursue a particular course of action and not its alternatives.

Costs use common units—that is, money—to measure the various inputs that produce a specific output (for example, trained people). For better or for worse, determining the costs of a program makes it possible to compare all such programs using a common unit of measurement. This does not imply that it is easy to determine all the resources needed to accomplish a particular training program, or that it is easy to obtain the direct costs of all resources. It may be possible to know, for example, only that the strength of a mentoring process is that it creates a positive image of the organization.

Effectiveness

The effectiveness of a training program is the extent to which people can do what they were trained to do. It is the output of the resources expended by a training program. Because the purpose of training is to improve performance and, to some extent, turn a novice into an expert, measuring effectiveness requires you to measure the amount of improvement in performance that a particular method of training (including mentoring) produces. Typically, effectiveness is measured by the amount of improvement in performance produced by a new method of training, compared to a previous one.

Problems concerned with collecting effectiveness data generally involve identifying the relevant measures of effectiveness (more than one may be required) and demonstrating that student performance measured in the test environment does in fact also occur later in the workplace or operational context. Collecting training performance data that satisfy statistical and analytical requirements is almost always difficult.

Cost-Effectiveness

Cost and effectiveness are independent measures of the input and output of a particular program. A comparison of the cost and effectiveness of alternative methods of training should yield the information a decision maker needs to make an informed choice among the options. For example, if two training programs produce equally effective results, the choice would be the less costly one. Or if two programs cost about the same, the choice should be the more effective one. Specifically, the cost-effectiveness methodology fixes the value of either the input or the output. If the input is held constant, we can compare two methods of training that cost about the same and select the one that is more effective. If the output is held constant (say, attrition is reduced by 20 percent), we can compare two methods of training that are equally effective and select the one that costs less.

It is always possible that some external factor that is not, or cannot be, included in the cost-effectiveness evaluation of training programs significantly influences the final decision. Sometimes external factors are rational (insufficient funds, changes in the economy, changes in ownership, a new chief executive officer). Sometimes they are not (outright rejection of mentoring, nonacceptance of simulations), even though they are clearly cost-effective. In any case, a cost-effectiveness evaluation can give guidance to a decision maker, but the decision maker must still decide what to do.

Cost-Benefit Analysis

A distinction should be made between cost-benefit and cost-effectiveness analysis. A cost-benefit analysis is one in which both the input and output values can be measured in monetary terms. This analysis requires an open market to assess the value (in monetary terms) of the outputs resulting from a particular use of resources (that is, the benefits). One example might be a cost-benefit analysis of a particular form of advertising. The costs are those needed to develop and conduct a particular advertising program; the benefits are the profits that may be attributed to the advertising program.

Cost-effectiveness analysis avoids the limitation of determining monetary values of both inputs and outputs. Clearly, however, if the data are available, a cost-benefit analysis is preferable because both input and output can be compared using the same units.

Value to the Organization

The value of any intervention is the extent to which it contributes to the success of the organization. This type of measurement requires statements as to why the intervention was initiated in the first place. Is it to increase production, retain personnel, or increase profits? The intent is most likely a combination of desired outcomes. For example, motivation, attitude, and skill development for an employee result in increased productivity and decreased personnel turnover. A facilitated mentoring process typically adds greater value than it costs in that it requires little in development costs and rarely results in lost productive time.

Measurement Considerations

Certain measurement considerations must be resolved regardless of the level of analysis (organizational impact or individual performance) or the type of measurement (products, end states, or process consistency of procedures employed).

The value to the organization is the information required that permits assessment of either cost-effectiveness or cost-benefit. The measures used to determine whether a process adds value must meet these criteria:

- *Validity.* Do the selected measures accurately measure what they are intended to (say, attrition, motivation, increased skills)?
- *Reliability.* How consistently do selected measures yield the same results under similar circumstances (do different raters agree)?
- *Generalizability.* How comparable are the results of the measures?

The values you decide to measure, the assessment instruments you select, and the approach decided on dictate to a great extent the findings you obtain. If you select attrition as a value, then your data are attrition statistics. They do not indicate the satisfaction or skills of the protégés. In practice, it is good to select a variety of measures to aid you in your decision process. The simplest approach is to reduce the measures or indices to the cost or monetary value; then you have a common unit. If possible, invest in more than one approach to increase the soundness of your judgment.

Ultimately the key question is, What information, presented in what format, is sufficient to permit the decision makers to make an informed choice? Let's look at some special considerations for answering this question in considering the development process of mentoring.

Special Considerations for Evaluating a Mentoring Process

A mentoring process is interactive and nonlinear. In other words, the protégé and the mentor interact, and they in turn influence and are influenced by other components of the organization. Further, these interactions and influences occur in a convoluted (if not chaotic) manner. Therefore, an assessment can rarely isolate a single factor or simply sum up several factors.

What do these facts suggest about how you design your process evaluation? You must not expect a single condition or measure to yield sufficient data for decision making. As has been discussed in previous chapters, the characteristics of both the protégé and the mentor must be considered. In particular, the leadership styles of a mentor may well have impact that varies with the type of protégé, and these results may vary according to context—that is, in a particular type of organization or in an unusual functional department.

An example of the impact of leadership style in different situations may shed additional light on this concept. A study of U.S. Army platoon performance (H. H. McFann, interview by the author, 1990) compared aptitude (intelligence) of platoon members, motivation of platoon members, and leadership style (directive or nondirective) of the platoon leader. None of the factors by itself was significantly related to platoon performance. However, results varied when the leadership style was combined with the other two variables. The nondirective leadership style was found to be most effective with high-aptitude platoons whether they were motivated or not. In contrast, directive leadership was found to be most effective when the platoon members were, on the average, lower in aptitude and were highly motivated. If they were not motivated, then nondirective leadership was most effective.

The message is simple. Straight overall assessments may not tell you everything you need to know. However, don't be discouraged. Your initial planning for assessment is a good start. My advice is to keep the evaluation process as simple as possible, relating it to the reason you considered the process in the first place. Here are strategies meant to assist you in undertaking this important and valuable activity.

Developing the Evaluation Plan

The first question to ask is, "What will we do with the data once we have them?" Then ask, "What do we want to know about the impact of our mentoring process on the organization?" Answers to these

questions are critical to the evaluation process. If you have no inten-
tion of changing the process, do not go through the exercise of
putting elaborate data-collection and data-analysis processes in place.
If you just want to know how happy it makes people to have the
mentoring process, a simple feedback sheet yields this happiness
index. If you plan to use the evaluation data to continuously improve
the mentoring process for increased effectiveness, you must isolate
each variable to the extent possible so that you know the impact it
has. Or you may want to compare the impact of the facilitated mentoring process with that of other development strategies. In this case,
some form of comparative analysis is called for. Such an analysis
requires collecting data on each strategy, the interaction of the strategies, and the impact of both on the results you are analyzing.

Your regular management reports and personnel records may
contain most of the data you require to evaluate your mentoring
process, particularly if you have a computer database with records
of education, training, and work experiences for your employees.
Alleman (1982) cites several performance measures that can be
compared to determine the long-term impact of mentoring: number of months in leadership positions on committees and task
forces, number of positions of responsibility in community and professional organizations, promotion rates, number of merit-pay
raises, turnover rates, productivity rates, and performance ratings.

Where do you start in developing an evaluation plan? At the
risk of sounding facetious, I say start where you are. What results
are you getting with the training and development interventions
that you now have in place? These are your baseline indicators.
Look particularly at executive development, management training,
supervisory training, technical skills training, climate change or
culture change, and ethnic- and gender-sensitivity programs. Look
at your projected human resource requirements, and determine
how well you are filling them through current development and
recruitment efforts. If no systematic evaluation is being done in
development programs, you might go back and look at your readiness assessment from Chapter Seven.

Next, list the results you imagine the mentoring process might have. On which of the following do you expect it to have a positive effect?

- Recruitment
- Retention
- Employee skills
- Readiness for higher-level responsibility
- Workforce flexibility
- Motivation of protégés
- Motivation of mentors
- Current costs of training and development
- Public opinion about your organization

Implementing the Evaluation Plan

Once you have your baseline indicators and an overall idea of the specific results you are evaluating, you can use the following guidelines to evaluate whether or not your facilitated mentoring process is achieving what you want in these areas.

Protégé Progress

Whether you include all those who wish to participate or just a target group such as executives, start by setting up a tracking system for the protégé participants. Here are some of the main items to consider tracking:

- Protégé profiles and current assignment
- Skills at the beginning of mentoring
- Start dates in the process
- Planned development

- Time spent on development activities
- Costs for development time away from the job, training courses, and other costs
- Reporting to be done

Both the mentor and the protégé may complete forms that record experiences and actions at agreed intervals during the process. Such forms amass facts, figures, and feelings for evaluation. Some organizations build this data collection into the responsibilities of the coordination team. Our current best practices include a monthly checkpoint with each partner in the pair, and a quarterly or semiannual experience exchange of active pairs. Both the checkpoints and the experience exchanges rekindle motivation, alert the participants that the organization expects some value added, yield actionable data for improvement, and produce results data for evaluation.

Having baseline data is important. If you do some type of developmental diagnosis in preparation for the protégé's development plan, you have a baseline for measuring increased skills and competencies once the mentoring relationship is officially concluded. For technical and general career effectiveness, the protégés may rate their job-specific skills on a custom-designed skill database, and also assess generic skills using the Personal Skills Map. The same assessment instruments may be used to get a before-and-after look at the data. One organization implementing a facilitated mentoring process during downsizing to create a highly skilled workforce and beat the competition collected data in this way: "Our protégés increased skills by an average of 61% for those specific job skills outlined in their Mentoring Action Plans. The protégés also showed gains in 9 of 11 of the life/career effectiveness skills" (Duncan, 1995, p. 3). Or you may ask both mentor and boss to rate the degree of change in the protégé's skills as well as the promotability of the protégé.

→ *Install a system to track the career progress of the protégés.*

Mentor Experience

You also want baseline data on the mentors in your process. Geiger developed a process for Douglass Aircraft that features mentor role definitions and measures; the process serves as a learning tool and a measurement tool (Geiger, 1992). A simple questionnaire will do. Some typical questions might be "How do you rate the usefulness of such a process?" "Do you see yourself having the knowledge and skills to be a successful mentor?" "Are the process requirements clear and concise?" Other subjects that might be covered are these:

- Knowledge and skills of the mentor relevant to selection criteria
- Mentor attitudes toward the organization and loyalty to it
- Career plans
- Expectations for the mentoring relationship
- Time invested
- Perception of mentor's responsibilities
- Discrepancies between what mentors are expected to do and what they are doing

Similar responses and reactions can be gathered periodically during the mentoring process and at the conclusion of each relationship. Unusual situations reported in checkpoint questionnaires can be clarified with follow-up telephone or in-person interviews by the coordinator. Comparison of the data from each point in the relationship gives you a picture of trends in the opinions of the mentors during the process.

→ *Find a way to track the mentor's attitudes.*

Recruitment and Retention in Target Group

Improved retention among the protégés is an oft-cited benefit of mentoring. Linda Pepin, senior vice president of human resources at Cabletron in Rochester, New Hampshire, says of mentoring: "It is a great retention vehicle. We have a reduced turnover rate. The company attracts and keeps talented employees" (quoted in Tyler, 1998, p. 100). To test this potential outcome, you must know the rate of turnover across the organization and for the target group prior to implementing the mentoring process. Tracking the rate of turnover for the target group is the easy part. Keep in mind that you must also analyze the reasons for the turnover. For example, a skillful mentor may help someone who is inappropriate for a job make the decision to leave that job. Isolating all the other variables that may have a causal relationship with turnover is difficult. At the least, you want to know how your turnover statistics compare with those of other organizations in similar industries or professions, both before and after implementing your facilitated mentoring process.

In addition to looking at the numbers or percentages, you must be aware of the monetary costs of turnover to the organization. Are people lost from critical jobs, where a vacancy means lost productivity or failure to provide an essential service to a client? What is the cost of replacement, including recruiting, hiring, orienting, and perhaps training new people? Christina Melnarik (1998) found that it was costing high-tech companies $577,000 to replace a first-year engineer. These baseline data, when considered with all the other variables, help you make an accurate assessment of the cost-effectiveness of the facilitated mentoring process.

→ *Capture statistics on turnover in the total organization, in the target group, and in other similar organizations before you start.*

Costs of Training and Development

If you have baseline data on the current costs of training and development programs, then by assessing the same costs after facilitated mentoring has been in place for a while, you can judge whether there is a cost reduction.

Calculating the costs of training is a challenge for everyone, even those with the most automated accounting systems. However, personnel database software is becoming comprehensive and reasonable in cost. Only a few years ago, the only computer programs for person-nel data ran on large mainframes with software costs running into five figures. Installation and data entry increased the costs significantly. Now human resource software for personal computers costs just a few hundred dollars. It can be installed with relational databases that gen-erate standard reports, including skill inventories and skills searches.

To capture the cost of training, begin by looking at the amount of time trainees spend away from the job while in formal training courses, a cost that is often obscured. The registration fees for external programs are even more difficult to isolate. These fees might be considered an education cost for the tuition, or a cost of travel. Related expenses for travel, accommodations, and incidentals may be reported as the cost of training, or they may be taken from a separate pocket in the budget. For more specifics on creating a defensive, cost-effective process, see the guidelines in Judith Hale's book *Performance-Based Certification* (1999).

→ *Calculate the costs associated with all the elements of training.*

Cost of Administration

The cost of staffing the coordination team is easy to track. Other administrative costs may be subsumed in the cost of maintaining the personnel department. It may be more trouble than it is worth to your organization to try to isolate such costs; however, a com-plete evaluation would include all available data.

→ *Establish a database for recording administrative costs of the mentor-ing process.*

Other Items

The duration of the relationships can be tracked by keeping records of mentor-protégé pairs, the dates the mentoring agreements were negotiated, and the dates they were concluded.

To continuously improve the process, record the issues reported by mentors and protégés. These comments can be invited in the interviews done with individuals or in the experience meetings conducted with groups of mentors and protégés.

→ *Set up a simple reporting process for both mentors and protégés at regular intervals.*

Checklist

Now you must decide how extensive you wish your evaluation to be. Once you have the basic evaluation outcomes in mind, go on to the checklist in Exhibit 13.1 to make notes on how to collect pertinent data.

Exhibit 13.1. Checklist for Designing an Evaluation of the Process.

Action to Take

1. Why did we start this process in the first place? _____

2. What do we want the mentoring process to do for our organization? _____

3. How do we define success for the mentoring process? _____

4. What do we do with the results of the evaluation? _____

5. What data must we have to make decisions about the future of the process? _____

6. How can we get the data we need? _____

7. What reporting is required or requested of
   • Mentors?
   • Protégés?
   • The coordination team? _____

8. What is our database capability now? _____

Other questions

9. _____ _____

_____ _____

10. _____ _____

_____ _____

Chapter Fourteen

Gender, Culture, and Relationship Concerns

Organizations are increasingly recognizing the business imperative of mirroring the customer base and the community in their workforce, at all levels. Shell Oil's mentoring process is designed for such current and future business needs. "We're building a candidate pool of more diverse leaders who may not be identified through traditional processes," says Leslie Mays, Royal Dutch/Shell's global diversity practice leader and a program sponsor. "Although most people think of diversity in terms of race and gender, it's much broader, involving . . . thought processes, problem-solving approaches and experience" (quoted in "Mentoring Mentees," 2000, p. 4). With the business benefits of diversity come some concerns.

Until now, this book has focused primarily on the practical aspects of putting facilitated mentoring processes together. This chapter deals with some of those concerns that people have about the mentoring relationship: gender issues, sexual attractions, crosscultural pairing, racism, and a potpourri of other problems that can occur whenever two people are brought together.

Gender Issues

Spontaneous attraction between two people can stimulate positive energy for both and result in increased productivity for the organization. An arranged match may miss this spontaneous surge of excitement yet still be productive by all measures. To make arranged matches work, the organization can identify multiple candidates for the mentor role and allow the protégé to spend time with each to see how the chemistry develops. Avoiding a serious mismatch is the responsibility primarily of the coordination team. The match must not be forced if either of the pair does not like or respect the other. In Hewlett-Packard's Roseville Plant mentoring process, protégés can even specify whether they would prefer someone of a certain race or gender, and they can change mentors if the relationship is not successful (Ferraro, 1995).

Allowing the protégé to nominate several mentor candidates and offering some tools for assessing skills, behaviors, and interests goes a long way toward increasing the likelihood of compatible work behaviors and personalities. Some of the concerns of managers are that mentoring relationships become too personal and emotional. A number of researchers suggest that facilitation of the pairing avoids some of these issues. When the mentor selects the protégé, the protégé may be reluctant to say no even when the relationship is not wanted. "Although favored for some aspects of the relationship, informal mentoring can sometimes leave a feeling of excessive dependency, a feeling of being constrained by having a more powerful figure breathing down your neck, and resentment from less favoured colleagues" (Clutterbuck, 1995, p. 2).

Like any close involvement, the relationship between the mentor and protégé has the potential to become personal and emotionally charged. The pair may discuss the potential for personal involvement, agree to maintain objectivity in the relationship, and then find it impossible to maintain the desired emotional or physical distance. Even if there is no romantic interest between a protégé and mentor, gossips often manufacture it. Mary Cassatt and Edgar Degas had a long-standing professional relationship—nearly forty years—and though both denied ever being lovers, rumors abounded (McMullen, 1984). More recently (and in quite another context), the notorious relationship between Bill Agee and Mary Cunningham at Bendix was given lots of press through all the stages of their working together, while they denied that there was any intimate involvement. The public interest in their relationship continues, even now that they are married to each other (O'Reilly, 1995).

Why do many people think that professional women, especially those who have fought long and hard for a promotion, would risk their careers for a romantic relationship with a mentor? The proliferation of special programs for women perpetuates the assumption that women do not know how to behave in the workplace. The message is that they are different (read: *deficient*) and therefore require remedial training. Look at the titles of the seminars and workshops marketed to women: Assertiveness Training for Women (offered by CareerTrack), Image and Communication Skills for Women (National Businesswomen's Leadership Association), What Makes the Difference: Success Strategies for the Promotable Woman (Management Training Systems), and on and on. Perhaps these seminars are popular because people believe that women inherently do not have the right psychological makeup for managerial roles. In a survey of training programs for women and men, Berryman-Fink and Fink (1985) found that organizational structures and management theories have traditionally been derived from the military and team sports—predominantly male spheres of influence. Compared with these macho models, the female seems to be a misfit and in need of special training. However, the role of mentor more often involves one-on-one activities than team plays.

Research suggests, however, that most women and men do not abandon all sense of propriety when they become mentor and protégé. A study conducted by Belle Rose Ragins and Dean B. McFarlin of Marquette University examines cross-gender and same-gender mentoring relationships. Among their findings: "cross-gender protégés were less likely than same-gender protégés to report engaging in afterwork social activities with their mentors" and "the potential of sexual involvement (which is increased with the intimacy component of friendship) may be less of an issue in cross-gender relationships than the simple appearance of involvement. The mere rumor of involvement can damage the relationship's credibility and, ultimately, the members' careers" (Ragins and McFarlin, 1990, p. 333).

Because of these prevailing beliefs, and in spite of some evidence to the contrary, cross-gender pairings continue to be a subject of special concern. One issue is the structure of the relationship itself. A common stereotype of the mentoring dyad is that the mentor will be male and the protégé a younger male. In fact, women who are seeking a mentor at a higher level still have to choose mostly from men.

Sexual attraction does occur in some mentor-protégé relationships. We all know people who have had sexual affairs with coworkers or bosses. Personal involvement with others is a fact of working life. Whether these relationships are harmful or helpful is open to debate. "Sexual attraction can't be stopped and it can enhance the organization. It should be managed so it has a positive, not negative, effect on the organization and its people," says organization development consultant Kaleel Jamison (quoted in Spruell, 1985, p. 21). However, Harrigan (1977, p. 287) says this will always be a no-win situation for women: "Business sex is guided and directed by a set of conscious and unconscious rules that are invariably beneficial to men and deleterious to women who work in the same corporate institution. *Women can't win this game.* They must not play . . . if they want to remain viable activists in the impersonal master game of corporate politics where the goal is money, success, and independent power."

To avoid the dangers of a sexual attraction in a male mentor–female protégé relationship, the pair often opt for a father-daughter form of behavior. According to Kram (1985, pp. 22–23), both careers suffer from this adaptation: "The woman who colludes in playing a helpless and dependent role forfeits the opportunity to demonstrate her skills and competence. The male mentor who maintains the role of tough, invulnerable expert forfeits the opportunity to ask for help when it would be useful."

Managers and administrators have traditionally tried to ignore office affairs, hoping they go unnoticed or go away. But they often also ignore reported instances of sexual harassment because they do not want to deal with the hot potato, and because they believe it is to be expected. Commenting on the implied contract of sexual favors in return for male sponsorship, Fury (1980, p. 46) writes, "I wouldn't say there's always an erotic aspect to such relationships, but it's there quite often. . . . How many times to bed equals one promotion?"

Suggestions on how to deal with the sexual attraction of people in the same office rather than ignore it have ranged from referral for counseling to ousting one or both of those involved. Most of the time, the woman loses her job. But perhaps we should not overlook the powerful energy exuded by people in love or in other emotional involvement. Einstein is reputed to have accomplished most of his creative work in three spurts—each of the three times he was madly in love!

Here are some guidelines that can be included in the orientation for mentors and protégés for handling the issues of personal attraction:

- Acknowledge the potential for sexual attraction, particularly in the closeness of a mentoring relationship.
- Discuss the organization's policies on sexual harassment, homosexuality, dating other employees, employment of related persons, and other such concerns.
- Identify the negative and destructive, as well as the positive, aspects of sexual tensions on the job.
- Specify the types of relationship that are absolutely taboo—for example, between coworkers reporting to the same supervisor, when one of the pair is reporting to the other, or when one or both are married.
- Describe the consequences of violation of policy and taboo.
- Establish the recourse available if either one behaves inappropriately in the relationship.

Another gender issue in mentoring is the belief that upper-level women do not help their female coworkers advance. This myth can be dispelled. Consider this quote from one of Bowen's study respondents who was in a female-female dyad: "I now move in an entirely different circle. I have even changed who I want to be. An enormous impact! She makes sure I meet people" (1985, p. 32). Bowen's study, limited to fourteen female mentor–female protégé pairs and eleven male mentor–female protégé pairs, clearly showed that it is not the gender of the mentor but the functions provided by the mentor that account for whether the protégé sees her career as on the fast track or not. Those functions involve using many characteristics traditionally described as feminine: caring, nurturing, and protecting.

In fact, evidence indicates that women may make better mentors for both male and female protégés. Internationally renowned anthropologist Ashley Montagu describes women's interpersonal skills as superior to those of men: "The female's practice of the art of human relations continues throughout life; and this is one of the additional reasons that enable women to perceive the nuances and pick up the subliminal signs in human behavior which men usually fail to perceive" (1974, p. 182).

Ellen Fagenson studied the needs of protégés for achievement and power and found that those who did become protégés differed from those who did not enter a mentoring relationship: "Neither individuals' gender nor the interaction of individuals' gender exerted a significant effect on their needs. Thus men and women who had become protégés had similar needs" (Fagenson, 1992, p. 56).

Cross-Cultural Issues

It always seems easier to make contact with and relate to people who are just like ourselves than to those who are not. In most U.S. businesses (and in government), the majority of senior managers and administrators are still white males. In this situation, the biggest problem with informal mentoring for the minority protégé is finding someone to develop a relationship with. Interacting with people who look different or behave differently takes more energy than some people want to give to a situation. As one protégé in a budding mentor relationship puts it, "It's not that people are prejudiced, it's just that they don't share a common experience. A white male is more likely to relate to another white male than to a Hispanic male like me. With someone from my own background, I don't have to explain where I'm coming from" (Wilkens, 1989, p. 2). However, mentors can also be intolerant and judgmental of those who resemble themselves, especially if their protégés make the same mistakes they did (Flaxman, 1990).

In the work environments of the future, there will be little choice about working with one group of people rather than another. The workforce is increasingly diverse. Women account for 47 percent of the 139 million workers in the United States, and two-thirds of new workers between now and 2008 will be African Americans, Hispanics, Asians, and other minorities (U.S. Department of Labor, 1999). Obviously, people must learn to live and work successfully with others of widely varying cultural backgrounds and needs.

This increasing diversity is all the more reason for facilitating the mentoring process because the organization can then deliberately pair mentors and protégés from dissimilar ethnic or cultural backgrounds to let them learn first hand the value of different approaches when teamed on a task. Such pairs face some unusual demands. Preparing the parties for successful cross-cultural relationships is a challenge for the coordination team, calling for them to find cultural learning experiences for the pair. One cross-cultural mentoring pair in California told me they went to a local museum a couple of times just to learn about cultural artifacts of people in cultures other than theirs.

In the early 1980s, many workshops and seminars on sensitivity training were made available to whites working with people of color (African Americans in particular). Obviously, organizations cannot continue to invent training programs to teach people to deal with every ethnic group in the country. But people can study the culture of those with whom they work and pay particular attention to the similarities and differences among individuals.

Understanding another group does not mean expecting less of them, however. George E. Curry, New York bureau chief of the *Chicago Tribune*, does not believe in special treatment for minorities (interview by the author, 1990). Curry, who has "mentored" numerous young people interested in journalism, says: "Some non-minorities have confided to me that, deep down, they have some reluctance about being 'too hard' on African Americans and other minority group members for fear of being labeled a racist. I think it's racist *not* to challenge minority students."

How can mentoring help to improve cultural exchanges in organizations? Acquisition of American companies by Japanese firms has brought the issue of cultural styles into sharp focus. American workers, who have operated under authoritarian managers, do not understand and respond to the team approach. A mentor who has experience with the other culture can help to accelerate the learning process. In many of these cases, combining functions such as payroll handling with personnel means that many experienced staff people at high levels are declared redundant. These people can be designated as mentors to teach new employees the ins and outs of the other culture (Zey, 1988).

What can a mentor do when the issue of racism in the organization comes up? Confront it and deal with it honestly. Curry (1990, p. 11), who works primarily with students, says that "if one is to have a meaningful relationship with a student, minority or otherwise, then one has to be honest, especially about the prevalence of racism. The minority student who hears from a mentor that racism no longer exists might question that mentor's candor. On the other hand, one can say, 'Yes, there is indeed racism in the United States and in many other countries.' Having said that, it is important to then add, 'You can beat the odds. You can become successful in spite of racism or discrimination.'"

Other Problems for the Mentoring Pair

As in all relationships, many complications and problems can come up. In previous chapters, I suggested strategies for preventing and remedying sticky relationship issues: periodic feedback to the coordination team; a no-fault conclusion; and a detailed, realistic agreement. These and other strategies can be used to deal with the most common relationship complaints.

Perception That Needs Are Not Met

As we have suggested, unrealistic expectations for the outcomes of the mentoring relationship can lead to growing hostility between the parties. But even if the mentor and protégé have discussed and agreed to specific outcomes and the relationship is amicable, the protégé can still feel that his or her needs are not being met. With so much contact and proximity, the mentor is an easy target and may be blamed for shortcomings that are, in fact, the protégé's. To counter this potential, the mentor can suggest that the protégé write out expectations (see Exhibit 12.1 in Chapter Twelve as a sample) and ideas for how they can be met as a start for resolving this concern.

Mentor Too Possessive

Feeling trapped by a possessive mentor who won't let go is a common complaint of protégés. Some are strong enough to negotiate themselves out of the relationship with no damage done to either participant. Others just drift along without initiating contact with the mentor, hoping the relationship dies a natural death. Sharpening assertiveness skills during the orientation of both mentoring partners may prepare them to handle this type of issue skillfully. If all else fails, the coordination team may have to intervene to convince the mentor to let go. Not all mentors are possessive, of course. One mentor told me that one of the most rewarding experiences of his life was seeing a former protégé promoted to a level above himself (T. Swift, interview by the author, 1989).

Personality Clashes

When mentors are assigned rather than mutually selected, it is easy for behaviors and styles to clash. Making participation entirely voluntary, employing multiple mentors, and giving the pair an opportunity for a get-acquainted period prior to negotiating the development agreement can decrease the likelihood that a match is made between people with totally incompatible personalities.

Protégé Too Ambitious

If the protégé is too close for comfort (organizationally speaking), the mentor may be reluctant to assist with further development ("Why develop my own competition?"). The ambitions of the protégé can also become an obstacle if they cause unnecessarily aggressive behaviors. For example, a protégé who wants to appear in the know might disseminate information shared in confidence by the mentor.

The coordination team may be asked to intervene if other career guidance might be useful. Skip-level mentors are less likely to feel threatened. The boss and mentor can collaborate on how to counsel a protégé on the realism of ambitions. Similarly, they can offer counsel on the consequences of violating confidence.

Some popular literature suggests that these problems do not occur in happenstance, informal mentoring relationships. This claim is not only romantic but untrue. All relationships have their problems. Our research found instances of sexual and emotional harassment in informal relationships, and the victim felt there was no recourse available. In one case, the mentor actually published under his own name a paper prepared by the protégé as a learning experience. By being aware of potential problems and dealing with them head on when they occur, an organization can have a facilitated mentoring process that is successful and long-lived.

Jealousy, Favoritism, Skepticism, Cloning, and Other Conflicts

In Chapters Eight and Nine, guidelines were given for selecting and preparing mentors and protégés for their roles in an effective mentoring relationship. Many of the issues that may arise between these two primary parties were discussed there, along with strategies for preventing serious problems. This section examines some other management and organizational issues and describes preventive action.

Jealousy

If the mentoring process is not clearly and openly publicized throughout the organization, it can provoke some emotional reactions from those who are not involved. Some protégés in informal relationships have felt that a facilitated mentoring process would have lessened the amount of jealousy they experienced when others suspected they were getting special treatment from a mentor (P. Schaub, interview by the author, 1990).

Even when processes are openly publicized, those people who are not participants may be jealous of the protégés. "Fast-trackers," "fair-haired boys," and "jet jobs" are labels attached to those who are known to be considered promotable, especially when they are engaged in special development activities. Your best strategy to keep this symptom from jeopardizing the process is to make the process parameters and selection criteria clear. Explain to nonparticipants how they can become involved and stress the choices they have.

Also, the direct subordinates of a mentor may be jealous of their boss spending time with a protégé from another part of the organization. Mentors may be suspected of neglecting their own employees when their protégés are outside the unit. This suspicion may be unfounded. Asked what effects, if any, participation in the mentoring relationship had on relationships with other subordinates, one executive at Federal Express replied, "I'm not taking time away from anyone in my organization" (quoted in Avant and Crosby De Berry, 1985).

Perception of Favoritism

Labor unions or other groups that represent employees may object to targeting specific individuals for future managerial positions. A good strategy for heading off interference is to invite employee

representatives to participate in designing the criteria and procedures for the process.

It appears that some unions are now taking a positive view of
training and development opportunities offered to employees. In
one manufacturing plant where I was a consultant, the union
pushed for a mentoring process for women to get them beyond the
first-line supervisor jobs. In General Motors plants (John Furman,
interview by the author, Apr. 25, 1990), dislocated workers are
offered one-on-one coaching and counseling on career opportunities, and funded training in basic skills, technical skills, and personal skills. Their union, the United Automobile Workers, is said
to be strongly supportive of these training and development
processes for the people they represent.

Skepticism

If members of an organization are not engaged in development
activities for themselves, they tend to be skeptical of the value of
all human resource activities ("I don't need—or want, or get—
special training, so why are we spending money on development
programs such as mentoring? It ought to be going for newer
equipment. What is the bang we're getting for the bucks we're
spending on this process?"). This kind of concern is a driver for a
sound evaluation plan, which was discussed in Chapter Thirteen.

Fear of Cloning

The fear that everyone will look alike, think alike, and behave in
similar ways as they are being mentored by a few top managers can
create resistance to formalizing the process. The stage play and film
How to Succeed in Business Without Really Trying carried this point
to its extreme by presenting the ludicrous picture of executives literally lockstepping through the office. Many an organization has
projected a corporate identity through the apparel of the executives.

The logo-printed school tie is still worn by many European executives. On flights today I often see the casually dressed young executive with a shirt sporting the company logo.

It used to be said that a powerful person (assumed to be male) looks at a potential protégé and sees a younger version of himself. But as Rosabeth Moss Kanter says, "Who can look at a woman and see themselves?" (1977, p. 184). With an increasingly diverse workforce, gender and ethnicity are strong factors that negatively influence the tendency toward cloning.

A research study conducted by Alleman (1982) found that mentors and their protégés in her experimental group were no more alike in either personality or background than the pairs in her control group of nonmentors and their subordinates. Mentors did not select the same adjectives (from a list of three hundred) to describe themselves and their protégés any more often than nonmentors in the control group did. However, protégés did describe themselves and their mentors through using the same terms. Apparently the protégés perceived a similarity to their mentors that either did not exist or was not perceived by the mentors.

Conflicts with Other Development Programs

When mentoring is set up as a separate, special program, it has to compete with other development programs for resources of all kinds. The sooner the process is integrated with other development programs, the less likely this conflict is to occur.

Checklist

As you review and make your notes on the checklist in Exhibit 14.1, you list preventive actions for dealing with the potential obstacles of gender, culture, and other relationship and organizational issues that may occur in your facilitated mentoring process.

Exhibit 14.1. Checklist for Identifying Gender, Culture, and Relationship Concerns.

Action to Take

1. What guidelines are given for cross-gender relationships? _____

2. How do we prepare mentors and protégés who are from different educational backgrounds, age groups, races, or cultures? _____

3. What measures can be taken to ensure that the protégé's needs are being met? _____

4. How can we minimize personality clashes? _____

5. What can be done to avoid the mentor's possessiveness from getting in the way of being a good mentor? _____

6. If criticism of the program arises because of relationship problems, what tactic will we take? _____

7. What will we do to minimize subordinate jealousy? _____

8. How do we publicize the program to nonparticipants? _____

9. How do we collaborate with labor unions or other employee representatives? _____

10. What do we do to prove the worth of development? _____

11. What can be done to avoid cloning? _____

12. What other conflicts do we anticipate, and what can we do to avoid having them jeopardize our program? _____

Other questions

13. _____   _____

14. _____   _____

15. _____   _____

Chapter Fifteen

Making Facilitated Mentoring Work

In the preface, I acknowledged being a lot smarter today than when I wrote the first edition of this book. The credit for this learning goes to all of my associates and clients who have shared their experiences with me. At the International Society for Performance Improvement (ISPI) Solutions Summit in November 1999, I described the best practices and lessons learned from my research and work with mentoring processes in seventeen countries. In this chapter, I recount some of the ways those organizations, and others cited in publications, are making mentoring work to improve results and achieve their goals.

In the first edition, I cited an article titled "Take My Mentor, Please!" by Peter Kizilos, which appeared in the April 1990 issue of *Training* magazine. This well-written article contained some horror stories about formal mentoring programs: mentors and protégés haphazardly thrown into relationships and left to manage on their own; mentors and protégés not speaking to each other; mentors sabotaging their protégés' careers. According to the article, many organizations use mentoring only as a quick fix. They do not have the culture or the internal support to make such a process successful over the long haul.

I'm pleased in this edition to cite another article from *Training*, "Mentoring in Changing Times," by Frank Jossi (1997). Here are some quotes to illustrate how three organizations in which Jossi conducted interviews made mentoring work successfully:

- "Managers and executives maintain formal arrangements with staff members outside of their supervision to discuss work-related issues at least once a month." (DuPont)

- "The program begins with a two-day training session that teaches mentors and protégés what to expect from the relationship and how to get the most out of it." (Texas Commerce Bank)

- "Mentoring has a just-in-time coaching aspect useful to less experienced employees. When confronted with a difficult conflict, for instance, they can call mentors for a quick dose of advice." (American Family Insurance)

Our research and practice continues to improve facilitated mentoring processes and develop preventive actions for potential pitfalls (Murray, 1999c, p. 561). One frequently asked question is how to avoid conflict between the boss and the mentor. Clear communication of roles and responsibilities all along avoids this pitfall. Debbie Darling, of Allstate Insurance, agrees: "Although the establishment of a mentoring relationship is not a replacement for the traditional role that managers play in the development of their employees, the organization hopes that its mentoring program will help employees to build their skills and increase their contributions to the organization" (quoted in Murray, 1999a, p. 224). Large organizations are often concerned about how to avoid having the mentoring process seen as exclusive. As Melana Borovich, of the Royal Bank of Canada, reports: "The issue was how to give all employees an equal opportunity to network. The selected strategy was a formal mentoring process for men and women in a number of different functions in the bank. The network that was subsequently created provides a variety of options in placing people in order to achieve the greatest effectiveness and efficiency for the bank as well as greater worker satisfaction" (quoted in Murray, 1999a, pp. 224–225).

Currently, mentoring is being used in many schools and charitable organizations to supplement resources and bring care and nurturing to those who need it. It is a fast-growing trend that is enjoying great success in these areas. The most important beneficiaries of mentoring relationships are young people. Every day in the media, we see public figures talking about the value of being a mentor to a child. I heartily endorse those messages and support local youth and student mentoring processes as a volunteer and advisory board member.

Some argue that businesses in the United States emphasize individual effort too much for mentoring to work; people believe in getting to the top without help. We do not have the patience of the Japanese or the true team spirit of the Scandinavians. The assumption is that greed and self-serving motives are rampant in American corporations. Meanwhile, divorce statistics in the United States prove that we are becoming worse at managing relationships. The question is, if we can't make a relationship work at home, how can we make one work in our business lives?

Some seasoned managers are optimistic that we can change the typical reactive behavior of U.S. business leaders. To do so, we must develop the patience and persistence to see programs that encourage change in organizational structure and in behavior fully implemented, and the ensuing benefits realized. Only with persistence can we reap the potential good results of concepts such as total quality, self-managed work teams, and facilitated mentoring. Beverly Kaye and Betsy Jacobson describe the payoff of new mind-sets for mentoring, such as groups or networks, including accelerated growth among high performers, new networks of peers, and a widening group of individuals who understand the power of intentional learning (Kaye and Jacobson, 1996). Denise Bolden Coley, a member of the task force in a mentoring program within Apple Computer, concludes that "the main goal is that the mentoring program, whatever form it takes, become a permanent part of the company's culture" (Coley, 1996, p. 48).

In reality, some organizations and some people will never be ready for mentoring. Facilitated mentoring processes won't work for everyone. But in the course of writing this book, we heard far too many success stories to believe that facilitated mentoring will go the way of trendy workshops and power suits. Chip Bell claims that mentoring often fails within an organization because human resource managers rush into what they think is a mentoring program, which instead turns out to be an overload of forms and procedures. Here's the advice

Bell gives to someone asking how to begin a mentoring program: "Let's figure out how to make mentoring as natural as calling a meeting and as institutionalized as budgeting" (Bell, 1996a, p. 138).

Both formal and informal mentoring have helped to create some outstanding administrators, managers, writers, artists, educators, and citizens. Exhibit 15.1 is a quick reference of the features

Exhibit 15.1. Comparison of Informal and Facilitated Mentoring on Key Success Factors.

Key Success Factors	Informal Mentoring	Facilitated Mentoring
Linked to business goals and needs	Mentoring not tied to goals; relationships not tracked	Linked to existing business initiatives; results are measured
Internal ownership of process	Ownership unclear; little support or coordination	Supported by project coordinator(s) who are skilled in communication, negotiation, mediation, and evaluation
Aimed at developing protégé's skills and behaviors	Often more generalized relationship; less specific focus	Focused on skill development and transfer of experience; also linked to individual development plan
Comprehensive orientation of protégés and mentors	No orientation; generic training, not linked to specific needs of pairs	Comprehensive orientation to focus on roles, key success factors, mentoring process, and goals
Ongoing support for mentoring pairs	No structured support	Coordinators facilitate, mediate, and provide resources as needed
Results are measured	Little or no follow-up; mostly anecdotal data	Baselines established during needs assessment; periodic evaluations measure results; results are linked to business goals

of informal and facilitated mentoring processes, with a comparison of what our best practices reveal to be the key success factors for a mentoring process.

If you are asked to implement a mentoring process, be sure to ask, "What is the gap?" Then do a thorough readiness assessment. It takes time, and it is worth it. Luis Gasparotto and Raúl Hornos (2000) interviewed twenty-two hotel managers and members of eighteen executive teams in Starwood Hotels and Resorts in Latin America to verify that mentoring was the appropriate intervention for their management development system (MDS), so that the organization could grow and compete. The continuing success of the MDS justifies the investment.

When you know your organization is ready for facilitated mentoring, prepare a careful design. Your entries on the checklists at the end of each of the chapters in Part Two give you the data you must have to construct your plan. Here is a checklist of the most important points to consider in your advance planning:

- Ask yourself why a mentoring process is needed; what is the gap that such a process will fill?
- State the desired outcomes for the process in specific, measurable terms. Specify benefits expected for the organization, mentors, and protégés.
- Assess the readiness of your organization to invest in a long-term process for facilitating mentoring. Is there support from the top and throughout the organization for the two or three years necessary to permit full integration and evaluation?
- Develop an evaluation plan to measure the impact of mentoring on the organization, the mentors, and the protégés.
- Determine where to place the mentoring function in the organization for administration and reporting.
- Select and train the coordinator or coordinators.
- Prepare a communication plan; then develop the materials to publicize the process.

- Design the structure and operating procedures for the process. Mentor and protégé identification, selection, orientation, and reporting strategies are the core components of these procedures. Be flexible in your approach.
- Execute the pilot process, gathering data to evaluate and revise as indicated.
- Use your evaluations positively and realistically to make continuous quality improvements to the process design.

The mentoring process must grow and change with the priorities and the people needs in the organization. Frequent scans of the organization environment, internal and external, give you clues as to when the business drivers demand different priorities for participating groups.

Finally, a request. When you have data on your experiences with facilitating your mentoring process, write them up and get them published! Your success story can save someone else time, effort, and money. Reinventing the wheel is not good use of anyone's time. Every day brings us new challenges in developing people. Our combined knowledge and experiences can ensure healthy work environments and happy, productive people.

Resource: Sources of Instruments for Assessing Growth and Development

20/20® Insight GOLD
Performance Support Systems, Inc.
The Bridgewater Group
100 Whitethorne Drive
Moraga, CA 94556

Career Planning Workbook
MMHA The Managers' Mentors, Inc.
2317 Mastlands Drive, Suite A
Oakland, CA 94611
Available in English, French, and Spanish

I-Sight®
Inscape Publishing
P.O. Box 59159
Minneapolis, MN 55459

Managing Personal Growth
Blessing/White, Inc.
900 State Road
Princeton, NJ 08540

Mentoring Resource Kit
MMHA The Managers' Mentors, Inc.
2317 Mastlands Drive, Suite A
Oakland, CA 94611

Personal Profile System®
Inscape Publishing
P.O. Box 59159
Minneapolis, MN 55459
Available in paper and electronic report format in several languages

Personal Skills Map™
Darwin Nelson and Gary Low
Emotional Learning Systems
6050 Rio Vista Drive
Corpus Christi, TX 78412
Printed and distributed by MMHA The Managers' Mentors, Inc.
Available in English, Spanish, and French

SKILLSCOPE®
Center for Creative Leadership
P.O. Box P-1
Greensboro, NC 27402

References

Adams, S. *Dilbert*. United Feature Syndicate. Sept. 7, 1994.

Alleman, E. J. "Getting a Handle on Mentoring: It Can Be Measured and Managed." Unpublished manuscript, Mentor, Ohio, 1982.

Avant, L., and Crosby De Berry, L. "Survey to Evaluate the FEC Mentoring Program." Unpublished survey and videotape. Memphis, Tenn.: Federal Express, 1985.

Bandura, A. *Social Foundations of Thought and Action*. Upper Saddle River, N.J.: Prentice Hall, 1986.

Bell, C. "Make Mentoring a Way of Life." *Training*, Oct. 1996a, p. 138.

Bell, C. *Managers as Mentors*. San Francisco: Berrett-Koehler, 1996b.

Berryman-Fink, C., and Fink, C. R. "Optimal Training for Opposite-Sex Managers." *Training and Development Journal*, 1985, 39, 26–29.

Blake, J. "The Bottom Line: Metrics and Survival." *On the Horizon*, Fall 1999, p. 3.

Blotnick, S. *The Corporate Steeplechase: Predictable Crisis in Business Career*. New York: Facts on File, 1984.

Bowen, D. D. "Were Men Meant to Mentor Women?" *Training and Development Journal*, 1985, 39, 31–32.

Brockbank, A., and Beech, N. "Feature: Mentoring." *People Management*, May 5, 1999, pp. 53–54.

Carmichael, J. M. "Demographic Impact on the Federal Employer." In *Conference Proceedings of the Nation's Workforce: Year 2000*. Milwaukee: University of Wisconsin, 1988.

Cavazos, L. F. "Cavazos Supports Mentoring Programs." In *A Special Report on Mentoring*. Pittsburgh: PLUS and National Education Association, 1990.

Clutterbuck, D. "Getting the Mentoring Balance Right." Letter to the Editor, Institute for Personnel and Development Journal, July 27, 1995, p. 2.

Coley, D. B. "Mentoring Two-by-Two." *Training and Development Journal*, 1996, 50, 46–48.

Collins, E.G.C., and Scott, P. "Everyone Who Makes It Has a Mentor." *Harvard Business Review*, 1978, 56, 217.

Corbin, B. "NOW Supports Researcher in NIH Sex Discrimination Suit." *National NOW Times*, Apr. 1994, p. 5.

Crosby, L. "How to Bring Mentor and Protégé Together—Formally." In *Report 1564, Sec. 1: Bureau of Business Practice*. Waterford, Conn.: National Foremen's Institute, 1984.

Crosby, L. "Mentoring at Work in Federal Express Corporation." *Manager's Mentor*, 1987, *1*(2), 4.

Curry, G. E. "Aim High." In *The Power of Mentoring*. New York: One PLUS One, 1990.

Darling, D. "Mentoring." *Peaks and Plains*, Fall 1997, pp. 12–13.

Dinnocenzo, D. A. "Labor-Management Cooperation: Keys to Success." In *Conference Proceedings of the Nation's Workforce: Year 2000*. Milwaukee: University of Wisconsin, 1988.

Dolainski, S. "Sage Presence." *Your Life Resource*, www.yapa.com, June 30, 2000.

Dole, E. "State of the Workforce." Speech given to the American Society for Training and Development, Orlando, May 1990.

Duncan, M. "Mentoring Applied." *Manager's Mentor*, Fall 1995, pp. 1–3.

Dyrness, C. "Group Mentoring Offers Small Businesses an Option." *East Bay Business Journal*, July 4, 1997, p. 8.

Eby, F., and Arrowood, C. G. *The History and Philosophy of Education: Ancient and Medieval*. Upper Saddle River, N.J.: Prentice Hall, 1940.

"EEO Works at NRC: Just Ask Cynthia Dekle." *Mentoring Connection*, Winter 2000, p. 1.

Ehrich, L. C., and Hansford, B. "Mentoring: Pros and Cons for HRM." *Asia Pacific Journal of Human Resources*, 1999, *37*(3), 92–107.

Everitt, S., and Murray-Hicks, M. "Models, Mentors, and Sponsors for Managers." Paper presented at the National Society for Performance and Instruction Conference, Montreal, Mar. 1981.

Fagenson, E. "Mentoring: Who Needs It? A Comparison of Protégés' and Non-Protégés' Needs for Power, Achievement, Affiliation, and Autonomy." *Journal of Vocational Behavior*, 1992, *41*, 48–60.

Farren, C., Gray, J. D., and Kaye, B. *Mentoring: A Boon to Career Development Personnel*. New York: American Management Association, 1984.

Ferraro, C. "Employees Learn the Ropes with a Little Inside Help." *Sacramento Bee*, Mar. 9, 1995, pp. 8–9.

Flaxman, E. "Good Mentoring." In *The Power of Mentoring*. New York: One PLUS One, 1990.

"Formal Mentoring Program Pays Off." *San Francisco Examiner*, Oct. 20, 1996, p. 11.

Fury, K. "Mentor Mania." *Savvy*, Apr. 1980, pp. 42–47.

Garcia, J., and McCrary, M. "How General Motors Implemented a Successful Workplace Mentor Program." *ASTD Reporter*, Golden Gate Chapter, 1997, *41*(5), 1.

Gasparotto, L. and Hornos, R. "Identification of Needs, Goals, Opportunities, Readiness." Paper presented at Making Facilitated Mentoring Work, panel presentation for the International Society for Performance Improvement, Cincinnati, Apr. 13, 2000.

Geiger, A. "Measures for Mentors." *Training and Development Journal*, 1992, 46, 65–67.

Glazer, R. R., and Murray, M. "Mentors: Myth, Magic or Manageable Development Model?" Paper presented at the Best of America Conference, New York, Jan. 1990.

Granfield, M. "'90s Mentoring: Circles and Quads." *Working Woman*, Nov. 1992, p. 15.

Gunn, E. "Mentoring: The Democratic Version." *Training*, Aug. 1995, pp. 64–67.

Halatin, T. J. *Why Be a Mentor? Part 3*. Minneapolis: 3M, 1989.

Hale, J. *Performance-Based Certification: How to Design a Valid, Defensible, Cost-Effective Program*. San Francisco: Jossey-Bass, 1999.

Harrigan, B. L. *Games Mother Never Taught You*. New York: Rawson Associates, 1977.

Heins, N. L. "Our Customers, Our Mentors." *Mentoring Connection*, Nov. 1995, pp. 1–2.

Hennig, M., and Jardim, A. *The Managerial Woman*. New York: Anchor Books, 1977.

Hooper, D. "We Are All Mentors." *Mentor and Protégé*, July 1990, pp. 1–9.

"Inexpensive MD-Nonprofits Look to Nontraditional Development Sources." *Management Development Report*, Spring 1992, p. 4.

International Society for Performance Improvements. "Making Connections." Conference program announcement, International Society for Performance Improvement, 2000.

Jossi, F. "Mentoring in Changing Times." *Training*, Aug. 1997, pp. 50–54.

Kanter, R. M. *Men and Women of the Corporation*. New York: Basic Books, 1977.

Kaye, B., and Jacobson, B. "Reframing Mentoring." *Training and Development Journal*, 1996, 50, 44–50.

Kirby, P. "The Trinity College Mentor Program." Unpublished manuscript, Trinity College, 1989.

Kizilos, P. "Take My Mentor, Please!" *Training*, Apr. 1990, pp. 49–55.

Kleiman, C. "Boost up the Corporate Ladder." *Chicago Tribune*, July 28, 1991, p. PC2.

Kram, K. E. *Mentoring at Work*. Glenview, Ill.: Scott, Foresman, 1985.

Laabs, J. "Hewlett-Packard's Core Values Drive HR Strategy." *Personnel Journal*, Dec. 1993, pp. 38–48.

Levinson, D. *Seasons of a Man's Life*. New York: Knopf, 1986.

Limerick, B., Heywood, E., and Daws, L. *Mentoring: Beyond the Status Quo?* Brisbane, Australia: Queensland Department of Tourism, Small Business and Industry, 1994.

"Margins to the Mainstream: An Action Agenda for Literacy." National Literacy Summit, www.nifl.gov, September 8, 2000.

McMullen, R. *Degas: His Life, Times, and Work.* Boston: Houghton Mifflin, 1984.

Melnarik, C. S. "Retaining High-Tech Employees: Constructive and Destructive Responses to Job Dissatisfaction Among Engineers and Other Professionals." Doctoral dissertation, Walden University, May 1998.

"Mentoring Mentees." *New Dimensions,* Winter 2000, pp. 3–5, 13.

Million Dollar Round Table. "Building a Team Through Mentoring." *Round the Table,* Nov.-Dec. 1994, pp. 24–25.

Montagu, A. *The Natural Superiority of Women.* New York: Macmillan, 1974.

Morita, A. "Education in a Changing Society." Paper presented at the International Federation of Training and Development Organizations conference, Tokyo, Aug. 1988.

Murray, M. "Upgrade Core Competencies with Mentoring." *Beta Gamma Sigma News,* Spring 1995.

Murray, M. "Mentoring Is Performance Improvement." *Performance Improvement,* 1998, *37*(2), 35–39.

Murray, M. "Coaching/Mentoring." In D. Langdon and K. Whiteside (eds.), *Intervention Resource Guide: 50 Performance Improvement Tools.* San Francisco: Jossey-Bass, 1999a.

Murray, M. "Performance Improvement with Facilitated Mentoring: A Global Perspective." Paper presented at the International Society for Performance Improvement Solutions Summit, San Diego, Calif., Nov. 1999b.

Murray, M. "Performance Improvement with Mentoring." In H. Stolovitch and E. Keeps (eds.), *Handbook of Human Performance Technology: Improving Individual and Organizational Performance Worldwide.* (2nd ed.) San Francisco: Jossey-Bass, 1999c.

Murray-Hicks, M. "A Behavioral Description of Mastery Performance of Professional Career Managers and of Graduate Students Entering the School of Management of John F. Kennedy University in 1976." Unpublished master's thesis, School of Management, John F. Kennedy University, 1977.

Myers, D. W., and Humphreys, N. J. "The Caveats in Mentorship." *Business Horizons,* 1985, *28*, 9–14.

Nanus, B., and Dobbs, S. *Leaders Who Make a Difference.* San Francisco: Jossey-Bass, 1999.

"Obituary of Dr. Benjamin Mays." *Richmond Times Dispatch,* Mar. 29, 1984, p. B2.

Odiorne, G. S. *Mentoring: An American Management Innovation.* Alexandria, Va.: American Society for Personnel Administration, 1985.

O'Reilly, B. "Agee in Exile." *Fortune,* May 29, 1995, pp. 50–74.

O'Reilly, L. "Mentoring Program Is Vital Part of Training." *Training Directors' Forum Newsletter,* Apr. 1989, p. 4.

Orlansky, J. *The Military Value and Cost-Effectiveness of Training*. Alexandria, Va.: Institute for Defense Analyses, NATO Defense Research Section, 1989.

PA Personnel Services. *Management Development and Mentoring*. London: PA Personnel Services, 1986.

Page, S. "Wanted: 100,000 Tech-Wise Teachers to Be Mentors." *USA Today*, May 30, 1996, p. 1.

Prange, J. A., and Smalley, L. "Becoming Your Own Futurist." In *Conference Proceedings of the Nation's Workforce: Year 2000*. Milwaukee: University of Wisconsin, 1988.

Premac Associates. "Mentoring Process Works Best When It Is Kept Informal." *Research Spotlight*, June 1984, p. 55.

Prism Performance Systems. "Just What's Needed, Just in Time." *Link*, 1994, vol. 2, no. 2, p. 8.

Ragins, R. B., and McFarlin, D. "Perceptions of Mentor Roles in Cross-Gender Mentoring Relationships." *Academic Press, Journal of Vocational Behavior*, 1990. Marquette University, vol. 37, pp. 321–339.

Roberts, A. "Homer's Mentor: Duties Fulfilled or Misconstrued?" *History of Education Journal*, Nov. 1999, pp. 81–90.

Robinson, S. "Mentoring Has Merit in Formal and Informal Formats." *Training Directors' Forum Newsletter*, May 1990, p. 6.

Roche, G. R. "Probing Opinions." *Harvard Business Review*, 1979, 57(1), 15.

Shepard, Y. "A Little Help from a Mentor." *Business Month*, 1989, 134, 15.

Small Business Administration. "Mentors Help Small Businesses Survive." In *Small Business Success*. San Francisco: Small Business Administration and Pacific Bell, 1990.

Spruell, G. R. "Love in the Office." *Training and Development Journal*, 1985, 39, 21–23.

Stiles, K. "Getting and Sustaining Leader Support." Paper presented at Making Facilitated Mentoring Work, panel presentation for the International Society for Performance Improvement, Cincinnati, Apr. 13, 2000.

Stromei, L. "An Evaluation of the Effectiveness of a Formal Mentoring Program for Managers and the Determinants of Protégé Satisfaction." Doctoral dissertation, University of New Mexico, 1998.

Stromei, L. "Awards of Excellence Spotlight." *ISPI News and Notes*, Aug. 1999, p. 4.

Sveiby, K. E., and Lloyd, T. *Managing Knowhow*. London: Bloomsbury, 1987.

Touby, L. "Do You Have a Mentor? *Glamour*, Mar. 1998, p. 172.

Trudeau, G. B. *Doonesbury*. Universal Press Syndicate, Oct. 28, 1984, p. 34.

Tyler, K. "Mentoring Programs Link Employees and Experienced Execs." *HRMagazine*, Apr. 1998, pp. 99–103.

U.S. Department of Labor. "The State of the American Worker." *Annual Report, Fiscal Year 1999*. Washington, D.C.: Government Printing Office, 1999.

Wilkens, M. "A Little Help from a Friend: Finding and Using a Mentor." *Pacific Bell Business Digest*, Oct. 1989, p. 2.

"Womanly Advice: Mentoring Works." *Holy Names High School Monarch* (Oakland, Calif.), Winter 1994, pp. 1–2.

Woods, E. *Training a Tiger.* New York: HarperCollins, 1997.

Zemke, R. "Using Testing Instruments in Your Training Effort." *Training/HRD*, 1982, *19*, 30–45.

Zey, M. G. "A Mentor for All Reasons." *Personnel Journal*, Jan. 1988, pp. 46–51.

Zuckerman, M. "Mentoring Has Merit in Formal and Informal Formats." *Training Directors' Forum Newsletter*, May 1990, p. 6.

Index

Process coordinators and coordination team. *See* Coordination team; Coordinators
Process goals and plan, 78
Productivity, increased, 34–35
Professional recognition of mentor, 67, 128
Professor Higgins, 53
Project Literacy U.S. (PLUS), 51
Projects, joint mentor-protégé: as benefit to mentor, 63, 67; credit taking in, 57; risk taking in, 68–69
Promotion and advancement: benefits of mentoring for, 47–48; frustration with mentoring and, 41; guarantees of, statement regarding, 41–42, 54–55, 173; jealousy about, 201; perception of favoritism in, 201–202; as reward for mentor, 67, 70; specification of, in agreement, 173; unrealistic expectations about, 54–55
Promotional materials, 126, 157
Protégé, 47–57, 131–144; ambition in, 200; benefits of mentoring to, 47–53, 131, 148; challenges of mentoring for, 53–57; characteristics of, 15, 135–137; commitment of, 42; criteria for, statement of clear, 132, 133; criteria for identification of, 132, 133; criteria for selection of, 135–137; developmental planning for, 137–143; goal specification of, in agreement, 169–170; matching mentor with, 78, 85, 94, 97–98, 99, 154, 159–160, 191–192; motivation of, 131; nomination of mentor by, 125; reports of, to coordination team, 164–165; sample calls for, 134; terms for, 15; tracking progress of, 185–186; who leaves the company, 42, 48
Protégé development planning. *See* Development planning
Protégé feedback, on mentor performance, 128
Protégé identification, 131–134; checklist for, 144; in Empire State College model, 99; in Executive Candidate Development Program (ECDP) model, 82; in generic model, 76–77; in RINA Accounting Corporation model, 89; strategies for, 131–134; in Trinity College Mentoring Program,

93–94. *See also* Matching mentors and protégés
Protégé responsibility, 45, 47; ability to take, as selection criterion, 136–137; for asking for assistance, 65; problems in taking, 55
Protégé selection processes, 134–137; bias in, 134–135; checklist for, 144; coordination team role in, 159–160; criteria in, 135–137. *See also* Matching mentors and protégés; Nomination
Protégé target groups: evaluation of improved recruitment and retention in, 187–188; succession planning for identifying, 103–106, 131
Public recognition, 68, 70, 128
Public sector hiring, 26
Public sector mentoring program model, 72, 83–86; graphic illustration of, 84; objectives of, 83; phases of, 83–86
Pulley, T., 34–35
Pygmalion effect, 52–53

Q

Qualifications, mentor, 117–123

R

Racism, 198
Ragins, B. R., 193
Readiness assessment, 74, 101, 103–114; checklist for, 113–114; of commitment to human resource development, 106–107; evaluation and, 177, 184; in generic model, 77; importance of, 207–208, 209; of organization's ability to sustain the characteristics of successful mentoring processes, 107–112; of scope of mentoring process, 107; of succession planning needs, 103–106; workforce projections and, 105–106
Real-time coaching, 65
Real-word education, 22
Recognition, for mentor, 67, 68, 70, 128
Record keeping, as coordination team responsibility, 154, 157
Recruitment, employee, 30; benefits of mentoring to, 36–38; tracking the impact of mentoring on, 187–188
Recruitment, mentor, 123–125, 153–154

Time commitment: for development,
106–107; of mentor, 66–67, 172–173;
for mentoring, 42; for mentoring versus "real job," 53–54, 140
Titles, for mentor role, 125–126
Tolerance of uncertainty, 22
Tosti, D., 122
Touby, L., 49
TRAC program. *See* Tumor Registrar
Association
Tracking, 42; of administrative costs, 189;
of duration of relationships, 189; of
mentoring relationships, 162,
164–165; of mentor's experience, 187;
of mentor's time, 66; of protégé
progress, 185–186; of retention and
recruitment, 187–188; of training and
development costs, 188–189; ways of,
111. *See also* Evaluation of process;
Measurement
Trainee, 15. *See also* Protégé
Trainer, 12
Training, 205–206
Training, defined, 5–6
Training programs: cost-effectiveness of
mentoring versus, 35–36; disenchantment with, 23–24, 40; integration of
facilitated mentoring with, 43, 86,
110–111; tracking the costs of,
188–189
Training workshops, mentor, 94
Trend extrapolation, 105
Trends assessment, 104
Trial period, 107
Trinity College Mentoring Program,
Washington, D.C., 36, 61, 72–73,
91–95; components of, 93–95; graphic
illustration of, 92; management and
structure of, 91, 93; objectives and
goals of, 91; protégé criteria of, 132
Tumor Registrars Association of California (TRAC) model, 73, 96–98; components of, 97–98; graphic illustration
of, 96; impetus for, 95, 97; objectives
and goals of, 97; policies and procedures of, 97; protégé nomination in,
132
Turf protection, 43
Turnover, 48, 188
20/20 Insight GOLD, 139, 211
21st Century Teachers program, 115
Tyler, K., 34–35, 49

U

Underrepresented groups. *See* Minorities;
Women
United Automobile Workers, 202
U.S. Army, 183
U.S. Department of Labor (DOL), 25, 28,
104, 146, 197
U.S. General Accounting Office (GAO),
26, 29, 80. *See also* Executive Candi-
date Development Program (ECDP)
U.S. Small Business Administration,
Office of Women's Business Owner-
ship, 33–34
University of Missouri, Columbia, 17–18
Upward mobility. *See* Promotion
Utility company mentoring program, 36

V

Validity, 182
Value to the organization, measurement
of, 181, 182
Valued added to education, 49
Voluntary participation, 108
Volunteer mentors: advertising for, 126;
as mentor recruitment strategy, 124,
125; response form for, 126–127; sam-
ple call for, 124
Volunteer protégés, 132

W

Wasko, C., 37
Welfare reform, 25
Welfare-to-work programs, benefits of
facilitated mentoring in, 39, 51–52
Wells Fargo Bank, Branch Manager MAP,
50–51
White males, as mentors, 196–197
Wilkens, M., 197
Williams, B., 137
Women, 10; affirmative action for, 24–
25, 30; benefits of mentoring to,
47–48, 49; discrimination against,
24–25, 135; facilitated mentoring programs for, 33–34; gender issues and,
191–196; as mentors, 195–196; prevalence of, in workforce, 197; as protégés, 193–194; stereotypes about,
193, 194, 195–196; on welfare, community mentoring of, 39; in workforce, 25